First published in Australia in 2014 by Heart to Heart Publishing
Address: 20 Ormond Rd Elwood VIC 3184
Tel: 0415-752311
Fax: 03-95313131
Email: andi_lew@yahoo.com
Website: www.realfitfood.com.au

National Library of Australia Cataloguing-in-Publication entry

Author: Lew, Andi.
Title: Real fit food : intelligent nutrition and functional training / Andi Lew; Gavin Ward, contributor.
ISBN: 9780987350466 (paperback)

Subjects: Nutrition, physical fitness, physical fitness--nutritional aspects, health.

Dewey Number: 613.7

Other Authors/Contributors: Ward, Gavin.

www.realfitfood.com.au
www.eatfatbethin.com.au
www.eatfatbelean.com.au
www.andilew.com

Cover photography by James Penlidis
Cover, layout and design by Felicity Gilbert
Edited by Julie Postance
Printed by BPA printing
Typeset in Georgia 11pt on 16pt

DISCLAIMER

All care has been taken in the preparation of the information herein, but no responsibility can be accepted by the publisher or author for any damages resulting from the misinterpretation of this work. All contact details given in this book were current at the time of publication, but are subject to change. The information in this book is provided for health education purposes and is not intended as medical advice. If you have any medical problems, please consult with a health care professional. The author and publisher shall not be responsible for any person with regard to any loss or damage caused directly or indirectly by the information in this book.

REAL FIT FOOD

Intelligent nutrition
&functionaltraining

Andi Lew

ABOUT THE AUTHOR

Andi Lew

Owner of Heart to Heart Publishing, Andi Lew is the co-author of the international top seller *7 Things Your Doctor Forgot to Tell You* and the natural parenting guide *The Modern Day Mother*. Her most popular best-selling books, *Eat Fat, Be Thin* and *Eat Fat, Be Lean*, have created a 'fat food movement' around the world.

A natural nurturer and advocate for healthy living, Andi Lew is a health professional, television presenter and owner of the Eat Fat, Be Thin Cooking School in St Kilda, Melbourne.

Andi is a qualified paediatric/infant massage instructor, Shiatsu massage therapist and an accredited Lifestyle, Food and Wellness Coach through Cadence Health and Wellness Coaching Australia. As the owner and director of Sipser Family Chiropractic wellness centre, which she ran for 12 years, Andi inspired thousands to live a better quality of life.

Andi has been an aerobics and fitness instructor in Club Med holiday resorts around the world, as well as health clubs and gyms in Australia. As a child, Andi obtained her brown belt in Karate and in 2012, she competed as a martial artist in competitions around Australia in Brazilian Jiu-Jitsu, the grappling and wrestling discipline.

As a result of her wellness lifestyle, Andi is often approached for advice on natural health and how to stay thin or fit post baby. As a TV and radio personality, she has presented on shows including *60 Minutes* and *The Today Show*. Andi writes on health for magazines such as *Ultra Fit, Australian Natural Health, Oxygen*, and *Cosmo Pregnancy* and blogs for model mum Miranda Kerr's *KORA Organics* website.

A dedicated mother and health educator, you can visit her websites at **www.andilew.com** and **www.realfitfood.com.au.**

A WORD FROM

HEART TO HEART

PUBLISHER AND AUTHOR,

ANDI LEW

This fabulous fitness book on feasting came as a result of the success of the *Eat Fat Be Thin* and *Eat Fat Be Lean* books in which the wonderful Dr Natalie Kringoudis was a co-author. From our books, a worldwide 'fat food movement' resulted.

I saw you become hungry for more information on exercise and fitness and I observed a real demand for fast and easy cooking. You also saw me take my training to another level and achieve new fitness goals with limited time to train.

I am now honouring your need to be fed more of the secrets - hence the release of my new book, *Real Fit Food*. Oh yes, and puns are intended! (*winks*)

Since opening my cooking school in St Kilda, Melbourne, many of you wanted recipes that were easy to make, fast to produce and would keep you looking fit. So, here we are, less than a year later, and with yet another brilliant book that will get you set for healthy eating.

This time I show you how to eat chocolate and ice cream so you will never feel like you are missing out!

I teamed up with sponsors, Cocofrio Ice Cream and PANA chocolate, because these treats are ones I have found to be foods you not only *can* eat, but really *should* eat because they're full of good fats and are free of sugar, dairy and additives. The good fats keep you happy and full.

I also collaborated with Dr Damian Kristof, Chiropractor and Naturopath, who is passionate about real food and real health. We both understand that real health is not merely the absence of symptoms or disease. Our wellness message is about achieving optimal function and living the life you were designed to. In these pages, you get knowledge on all things that keep you fit and truly well, and food that tastes amazing too!

01...................... **Foreword by Dr Damian Kristof**

05...................... **Introduction**

CHAPTER 1
13...................... Overfed and undernourished

CHAPTER 2
23...................... Lies we've been fed

CHAPTER 3
41...................... Hey sugar, we are over

CHAPTER 4
57...................... Fat and facts

CHAPTER 5
71...................... Functional training

CHAPTER 6
101...................... Real fit food planning

CHAPTER 7
108...................... Fast fool-proof recipes

108...................... **BREAKFAST IDEAS**
110...................... The breakfast cake
111...................... Caveman cereal
114...................... Kale omelette

TABLE OF CONTENTS

SNACKS 116
Hummus 118
Chia seed bread 119
Brussel sprout chips 122
Paleo crackers 123
Cauli flowers 126

DINNERS & LUNCHES 128
Moroccan spiced chicken 130
Green bean and broccoli 131
Pasta free Bolognese 134

SWEET TREATS 136
Chia puddings 138
Cocofrio ice cream spider 139
Choccy nutty crunch 142
Cuke and pine icy-poles 143

FESTIVE FOODS 146
Amazeballs 148
Cacao slice 149

DRINKS 152
Chocolate cashew milk 154
The LSD 155
Choc mint-tea 158
Coco coffee 159

foreword

What's better than getting the skinny on fat?

Learning a really simple way how and why some fats are really good for you! How cool would it be to devour an ice cream minus the guilt? Want to understand how to avoid sugar and which sweets are safe? You've always wanted a well-oiled machine of a body but just didn't know how to get your engine firing!

Over the last two decades you've been drowning in a bowl of confusion with messages of 'calorie-counting', 'quit sugar', 'eat low-fat' and all the next best diets with promises of this one being the one that works! You know you need to exercise, but you either can't stay motivated because you don't have the time, space or money. Or you are indeed exercising but you're not getting the results you had hoped for! Sound like you?

In this book, the third in the series, Andi Lew has yet again found a way of communicating an in-depth understanding of how your body works and what it needs to be amazing in a simple-to-understand message.

Teaming up with Crossfit Coach Gavin Ward, they have complied a fit guide to staying lean, strong and as you can see from their pictures, really healthy.

They help explain which exercises and movements are the best to do - like functional movements (where more than one muscle group is used at a time), so that you get a more effective workout which saves you time. As a chiropractor, I too recommend functional movement exercise programs, simply because we are designed to move this way.

Having been in the health and wellness industry for 20 years, I have seen a heap of health trends and fads come and go. I've seen people deprive themselves of vital nutrition in what I call 'natural quotient' or nQ. This stands for the natural intelligence in food. We have been tricked and robbed by clever marketing and we thought we were making healthy food choices, but the rise in heart disease and obesity in the Western world is becoming more rife.

What went wrong? If we are eating 'low-fat' and 'sugar-free', why hasn't it been working? The sad thing is we are getting more depressed and stressed than ever before and eating good fat and 'intelligent food' can actually help us cut carb and junk food cravings and give us more energy as well as lift our mood.

I've known Andi for many years and it's rare to meet someone with such an unwavering passion for health education. She has a unique knack for communicating complex messages in layman's terms and continues to research, rising above the rubble of poor-quality information. She sheds new light on the latest research and delivers quality information on individual health choices. As a 40 year old mother, her commitment to wellness is inspiring and you only have to look at her to see that she walks her talk.

After reading this book, you will feel liberated understanding the relevance of fats and sugars, nutritional assimilation and absorption and finally not feel so overwhelmed when it comes to what foods to buy in supermarkets. As an extra bonus you'll be able to 'have your cake and eat it too'. There's even recipes for 'real fit food' you can make fast!

Well done Andi, you've created a resource for any aspiring 'health nut' or athlete to enjoy 'bite-sized' chunks of insightful and entertaining information!

Dr Damian Kristof, *B.Chiro N.D.*

WHAT IS REAL FIT FOOD?

Introduction

"Hold up people!"

I hear you say. "What is 'real food' or even 'fit food'?"

"Why can I eat ice cream?"

Well it's not just any ice cream, but believe it or not, there are actually types of ice-cream and chocolates that are actually very good for you! We will learn which ones are minus the 'nasties'.

'Real' food is food that is nutritious. The more alive the food is, the more life it will give and have.

So it's not about the calories in food, portion sizes or quantity, but rather the type of calories and type of nutrition that is vital to keeping your body fit and healthy. If you consume food dense in vitamins and minerals, (micro-nutrition that comes from 'real' food), as well as fresh food that is full of antioxidants and life, you are providing your body with fuel that is essential and acts just like beneficial medicine.

It's really much easier to stay well than to get well and it's also a synch to stay fit and lean if you eat foods that are alive. Eating fresh foods that are full of life keeps our bodies running like well-oiled cars. This is vital if we want energy to train and burn that fuel.

Since the 1980s, we've been told that 'fit food' is 'low fat' food. We trusted in the dirty 'D' word - *diet*. We now know that 'low-fat' doesn't work. If it did, we would all be thin and we aren't. What's more, we are also exhausted. This is because 'low-fat' food is full of sugar. It's the sugar that makes you fat, not the fat. I'm referring to good fats, of course. Trans fats, which are man-made fats like margarine for example, *do* make you fat. But good fats that are in avocados, salmon, nuts, seeds and coconut oil for example, are vital for our overall health.

So how on earth do we eat well and stay fit while we have jobs and kids, you ask? This is the ultimate 'Modern Day Mother' dilemma! The answer is:

Do not spend too much time in the kitchen!

How much time is 'too much time' then? Well, less than ten minutes at a time to prepare is the answer. When you do spend time in there, make sure it's fun and get the kids involved. The recipes in here are easy, fail-proof and are that fast! They just need to be. After all, less time in the kitchen means more time in the gym or exercising, right?

So let's get our head and love-handles or muffin tops around the low-fat myth and say goodbye to 'low-fat' foods! Let's also get rid of dieting. We want your 'diet' to be your way of life, your lifestyle. You will feel so good and function so well, that you won't want to eat any other way, once you start to feel more energetic as you detox off the sugary foods.

Once, you've digested this concept, you will now be able to sink your teeth into just how much protein you should be eating, which refined carbs you need to say "sayonara" to and also understand that we will let you 'have your cake and eat it too!' Yup! There are some great recipes in here that allow you to eat cake and sweet treats without all the refined sugar every day.

How 'fit' are you?
Take the test!

1.   **Your fridge and pantry is full of:**

   a. Fresh organic non-GMO animal proteins, fruit and vegetables, raw nuts, nut-based milks, seeds, coconut oil, fermented foods and quality practitioner-prescribed supplements.

   b. Several conventional fresh fruits and vegetables, rice bran oil, non-organic fresh proteins, a couple of homemade leftovers consisting of muesli bars and pasta, wholemeal bread and supermarket-bought supplements.

   c. Low-fat, high sugar packaged foods, processed meats, white breads, cereals, canned and frozen fruit and vegetables, as well as margarine.

2.   Your friends would be described as:

a. Goal driven, positive and active go-getters and team players who call you regularly for a catch-up that usually consists of a walk and talk or a game of sport.

b. Supportive and optimistic people who constantly encourage you to join them on fun-filled adventures and new life experiences. You all enjoy learning the latest in fitness trends.

c. Procrastinators, who fill their free time with catch-ups over a beverage and a good belly laugh, follow by a sleep-in. They are happy-go-lucky and not too fussed over image and live life day to day.

3.   Your role models are:

a. Michelle Bridges, the trainer from The Biggest Loser show.

b. Jessica Simpson

c. Homer Simpson

4.   Your weakness at that time of the month or a midnight snack is:

a. A no-sugar, wheat-free, good fat filled homemade cacao, nutty bar.

b. Toast with high-sugar jam and a cup of hot chocolate.

c. A Toblerone chocolate bar, followed by a bag of trans-fatty crisps!

5.   Your best pre-workout snack before training is:

a. An organic banana, coconut water on hand and a handful of nuts and seeds.

b. A rice cake with low-fat cottage cheese and a herbal tea.

c. Coffee with sugar-free artificial sweetener and an empty stomach.

6. **Your next day recovery routine is:**

a. A gentle walk, ice bath, magnesium powder and a visit to your local chiropractor and massage therapist.

b. A gentle stretch upon waking, protein powder shake, and a social media status update about how sore you are!

c. A sloth-like day on the couch, or calling in sick to work, followed by 'reward food' at 'wine o'clock', ending with a social media status update that usually looks like this: *I'm never doing THAT again!*

Did you circle:

If you circled mostly A, congratulations! Give yourself a pat on the back! You are taking excellent care of yourself because you understand the importance of proper nutrition and exercise in your overall health and well-being, as well as quality of life and disease prevention. You understand the concept that your health is your wealth. You are well informed about health. You invest in seeing health practitioners regularly for wellness, and do not wait until you are sick to do something about your health. You are mostly likely never sick, always energetic, full of optimism, smashing through your goals and generally annoying everybody else around with your youthful glowing appearance!

You are however, a little 'OCD' when it comes to this area. But your efforts are inspiring to all those around you. Perhaps you should start acknowledging your achievements and stop to smell the roses on the way to the gym, once in a while.

Mostly B's

If you circled mostly B, well done! Your never-fading enthusiasm for health, makes anyone proud. You are a keen learner with good intentions and are always open to self-improvement. You mean well,

10

but are confronted with conflicting advice or information on health and nutrition in your search for wellness. Your state of health and general fitness is just above the average person and it means a lot to you to not only look great, but feel good too. You are a little bi-polar in your approach though, to-ing and fro-ing between 'amazingness' and 'can't be arsed'. To stay inspired takes a little more work and that is why this book will be great for you. The good news is, with some guidance and minor tweaking, you can be well on your way towards a super hero health fanatic and that role model photo you have pinned to the vision board you hide in your bedroom is about to become reality!

Mostly C's

If you circled mostly C, we commend you for your honesty, which takes courage. However, 'C' also stands for 'Care Factor: Zero'! You are in fact the reason we are inspired to do what we do! That's okay, we have all been there at some point too. This is all about to change. You have just begun a transformational crusade by reading this book and even though you have probably never really given much thought to the way you eat, rest or exercise, just know you are starting to care about your health and fitness. It's time to let go of old belief systems about diet and your old self-doubts. We believe in you and you can actually be the best you can possibly be. Who you are is wonderful and make sure you stay that way! It's going to be hard for you to put your hand in this pot of honey, without something sticking!

OVERFED AND UNDERNOURISHED

Chapter 1

"Let food be thy medicine and medicine be thy food"

- Hippocrates

Jason Vale from the *Hungry for Change* documentary summed it up perfectly when he said, "They want to sell you more food. They're into just selling and marketing." He was referring to the Food Industry and what food production has become.

In the past few decades we've been led to believe that we what see on supermarket shelves is food. Alright, some is but some isn't. In fact, 80% of food on supermarket shelves wasn't there before. It has become a 'fast food' array of colourfully packaged boxes, jars and cans all of which claim to 'tick all the boxes'. You will see clever marketing with all the key phrases you want to hear like *low fat, non-GMO, less salt, lite* and *gluten-free.*

But just because food is low-calorie or gluten-free doesn't mean that it is good for us. In fact, it is usually high in sugar if low in fat and will most certainly be full of preservatives or additives. If it is low in calories, it may be lacking in the type of calories, aka nutrition (and crucial nutrition at that) that we need to function at our full potential.

13

We have been eating lots of well marketed food. We have got sucked in to the messages claiming it to be 'good food' but we are severely undernourished and overweight or exhausted. In short, our bodies are starving for nutrients on a cellular level. We are 'dying' for some real food!

EAT REAL FOOD

Okay, so what is real food? It is food that is fit. 'Fit food' is food that is high in nutrition. Dr Damian Kristof, chiropractor, nutritionist and founder of Forage Cereals calls it 'nQ' which stands for 'natural quotient'. If the food is alive, plant based and organic, it will be full of life and nutrient dense. It has a higher nutritional intelligence and will therefore be good for us, and most importantly, our brains.

So try to eat as close to nature as possible and avoid genetically modified foods or fresh foods full of pesticides. Eating organic may feel like a challenge at first, but if you just incorporate a few foods, you may find that because the nutritional content is higher, you start using your food like fuel or medicine and you begin feeling a lot better. The food we eat can be the most powerful thing that can heal us – or poison us. So choose carefully. Let's try to understand 'organic' a little more.

Have you noticed how the label 'organic' is starting to take over supermarket shelves? The term 'organic' refers to foods produced in soils and environments that contain up to 5% of chemical residues and have no added pesticides or herbicides. Many people today are no longer willing to expose themselves and their children to what scientific research is revealing to be a widespread and growing pesticide health hazard. In fact, one major chain now has over 300 organic products, ranging from pasta to juice, canned foods, cereals, and even meat.

14

There are grocers and stores that specialise in organic produce popping up everywhere, and this is happening in response to increased public awareness and informed concern about the importance of nutrition. It is a growing and multi-million dollar industry for one reason only — demand. The demand for organic food has made it the new black in the food industry.

There was actually a time when the only food available was organic, because the chemicals didn't exist and food wasn't farmed the way it is now. People got their nutrition from food that was grown naturally and wasn't robbed of its vital minerals and nutrients.

What has happened to our eating habits? Our soils have been sterilised by the use of chemicals sprayed on produce. This is a major problem because much of the nutrients are passed from the ground where the plant is grown into the plant. Our modern foods are so full of hormones and pesticides that the nutritional and mineral content is questionable. Food industry adulteration and devitalisation has created the growing need for vitamins and supplements because we just aren't getting the nutrition we require from conventional foods.

For example, nuts are 'bombed' as soon as they enter the country. Huge warehouses full of imported nuts are drenched with pesticide bombs so powerful that the doors must be sealed shut to prevent the poisons escaping into the atmosphere. We can't breathe it, so why would anyone think we could eat it?

Organic food is so much more appealing nutritionally and tastes unbelievably different. It is a little more costly at the moment, but increased demand will inevitably bring an equalisation in price as more primary producers enter this increasingly lucrative market. And keep in mind that what you are presently saving short term in dollars by buying adulterated foods, you are losing long term in the negative effects on your mind and body.

Eating organically may sound a little daunting at first, but the best way to start is with a monthly shopping trip to your local organic or farmers' market, which is usually very affordable. Open up your senses and give yourself time to explore this new environment. Walk around and observe the different products available, try some of the fresh fruit and vegetable juices and taste the difference, and observe the different size, colour, scent and 'feel' of the vital foods there. There are many organic food delivery services now too, so there's really no excuse.

Understand that the organic fresh produce may not always be as pretty as the waxed apples or sprayed broccoli you normally see in a supermarket. Remember, the pretty appearance is achieved only with the use of chemicals that may have the same effect on you as they did on the insects and other organisms they exterminated. Combine that with the likelihood that the apples and oranges you buy have potentially been in storage for up to eight months. And it doesn't stop there. All produce at your local supermarket has been stored away. It's a nutritional disaster.

Broccoli is one of the most sprayed foods, so to make a big difference in your well-being you might like to start with the organic variety of this delicious vegetable. It will not only taste much better, but could end up saving you money in the long run as you appreciate it more, eat less, and require less supplementation.

Some organic foods may even surprise you with a worm lurking around in there. They may startle, but they won't harm you, and as long as you thoroughly wash the organic food, it's fine. Bugs are actually a guarantee of quality, because most insects cannot survive in foods that have been chemically treated, so if it's good enough for the worm to eat, it's okay for you as well.

You should actually be more worried that you *don't* find any worms on your normal food, as the harsh chemicals on the sprayed food have driven them away or killed them. What do you think the pesticide will do to you? The main thing is that if you are going to invest in eating organic, it too has to be fresh.

Is organic food healthier for us?

The exact nature and degree of the benefits of eating organic food have yet to be subjected to rigorous research, but anecdotal evidence abounds. At the very least, organic foods improve health because fewer pesticides, herbicides, waxes, and chemical fertilisers are used than in non-organic foods.

So is all organic food by definition a guarantee of health and reliability? No, unfortunately even here, you must remain discriminating and continue to take responsibility for your own well-being. The meat in an organic sausage may be free of antibiotics, but it can still be high in saturated fat, which raises your cholesterol levels and affects your heart.

Similarly, some organic biscuits and cakes may contain a lot of refined sugars which can lead to problems such as obesity, as well as some preservatives and additives (although the Soil Association and other regulatory bodies permit only a few). So let moderation be your guide with both organic and non-organic foods, and choose foods that don't come in packets.

Packaged foods usually have preservatives. Preservatives preserve.

Organic food is more natural, tastier, and helps keep you away from 'fast' and processed foods. This is because there is a part of the brain that recognises the higher nutritional content and switches off the hunger mechanism sooner. It feels more satiated from nutrition than volume. An example is tomatoes. You need to eat 100 conventional tomatoes to get the same nutrition as one organic one. Not only is organic food more nutritious, it reduces your intake of dubious and harmful chemicals that can have lasting negative effects on your health. Good food is not just healthy food; in many ways it can be a healing agent.

If you want more *life*, eat more *live* and *organic* foods.

Eat foods that are alive, not packaged — fresh fruit, vegetables and foods that grow.

When choosing more live foods in your diet, consider adding sprouts - they are new life. A sprout is the beginning of a vegetable, and will provide you with more energy as it is new life and bursting with growth.

Broccoli, apples and potatoes are often the most sprayed vegetables, so buy the organic versions.

Remember, if you don't like - or are not used to - eating vegetables, try the organic varieties as they taste quite different and better. You may find that organic carrots or pumpkin are actually sweet. If you can't taste the difference, detox from coffee, cigarettes and other toxicities to remove the coating from your taste buds.

Stay away from MSG (monosodium glutamate, 621). It is found in lots of packaged foods, is highly addictive and can make you hungrier. Although that will be the least of your worries; it is so toxic, it may also affect mood and cause depression.

Most importantly, get rid of your microwave! As easy as it has become to cook and heat foods this way, you may as well be throwing your good organic food away; studies have found that microwaves may destroy many of your food's vital nutrients.

> *"The doctor of the future will give no medicine, but will interest his patients in the care of the human frame, in diet, and in the cause and prevention of disease."*
> - Thomas Edison

Food is fuel

Imagine you have a Ferrari, or perhaps you already do. Would you put water, or dirt, or even regular fuel in the fuel tank? Of course not. In fact, you would use only top quality, high-octane fuel to get the best performance and longest life from your beautiful machine, and to reduce repair costs.

Well, your body is a Ferrari. It is unquestionably the most evolved, intricate and powerful vehicle on the planet; a brilliantly designed self-healing and self-regulating machine that is using everything you put in it to recreate itself every minute of the day. Putting poor quality or junk food into your body is exactly like putting inferior fuel into a

Ferrari. Your body is so resilient that even with the worst food it can still produce cells and continue to function, but the long-term effects of empty, non-nutritious foods are devastating.

Eventually the body can no longer adapt or compensate, with the result being disease and accelerated aging. It's strange that we would take more care of a man-made machine than a divinely created one, but we do.

So begin to think of your body as a Ferrari. Give it only the best fuel, and let it give you its best in return.

We are hopeful for a future where the history of medicine reads as follows:

"Doctor, I have an earache."

2000 B.C.	"Here, eat this root."
1000 B.C.	"That root is evil, say this prayer."
1850 A.D.	"That prayer is superstition, drink this potion."
1940 A.D.	"That potion is snake oil, swallow this pill."
1985 A.D.	"That pill is ineffective, take this antibiotic."
2000 A.D.	"That antibiotic is artificial and can harm you. Here, eat this root!"

So there's validity in saying, "Get back to your roots for more reason than one."

When you decide to juice your food, make sure that the juicer you use is one that masticates (squashes) the fruit and vegetables, so that unlike other conventional juicers where the motor heats up, your juicer won't kill off the enzymes in the food. This mastication process is one where it chews fibres and breaks up cells of vegetables and fruits, giving more fibre, enzymes, vitamins and trace elements. This method of juicing is highly recommended by the Cancer Support Groups and other health foundations.

Today, after decades of declining health and rapid ageing, the promise of living foods is once again gaining international attention simply for its natural healing properties and energy source. Living foods are an effective way of helping our bodies heal themselves. A healthy body is a body with healthy enzymes.

So fresh and raw or alive foods are the foundation of any healthy eating program, and have amazing healing and rejuvenating properties. They help improve immunity, increase energy, cleanse blood, promote vitality, manage weight, nourish organs and detoxify and maintain cellular structure.

The major benefits of a living food diet are that vital enzymes and nutrients remain intact and are able to be utilised by the body.

Juicing like this means we are preserving and maintaining high nutrition. And we need to do all we can to make sure we are getting maximum nutrients! You see, your body consists of trillions of living cells and we need living cells to feed them, which can only be found in living foods, easily assimilated as juice, or in other liquid forms. It just means you can ingest it effectively and your body can use it quickly.

Juicing is also a speedy way of helping the body to be more alkaline. Alkalising foods are foods that are mainly greens and of course nutritious and unadulterated. The packaged drinks we sometimes see or consume are acid forming. So things like sodas and carbonated varieties are mostly acidic inducing. It means your body becomes acidic -which can lead to a carcinogenic environment. If you eat lots of 'junk foods' and have an acidic environment, your body is more likely to be prone to inflammatory conditions and disease which thrive in an oxygen depleted system.

So eating as close to nature as possible means avoiding additives. Some packaged foods are okay and in fact very healthy for you. Take for example a packet of chia seeds - a wonderful superfood that comes in a packet. What you need to avoid though are packaged foods that have all sorts of additives and preservatives. These are usually nasty little buggers that are disguised as numbers on the backs of foods in the ingredients column. When looking for good food, try to use that as a guide. Too many numbers in brackets are a no-no and foods that don't have any are bound to be better! Food with additives do not 'add' anything to your life! It only means you're getting 'more calories and less nutrition'. It's the nutrition, or micro-nutrients that we need.

Also, be aware of what may rob the body of the nasties that rob your body of being able to absorb the great nutrition you will be consuming. Poor gut health as a result of too many medications, the oral contraceptive pill and even a poor working nervous system can impact your absorption and assimilation. So the best thing to do is to contact your healthcare practitioner and work together to get off the medication because this might be the reason you can't shift the last few kilos!

LIES WE'VE BEEN FED

Chapter 2

"The wise man should consider that health is the greatest of human blessings. Let food be your medicine."

- Hippocrates

We are up to our eyeballs with myths, stuffed with clever marketing and fed up with confusing labels and information. So let's set the record straight. Let's finally clear up any misconceptions you may have had about diets, how to lose weight and what is correct to eat if you want to be truly healthy.

MYTH No.1

Diet

Don't go on one! Create healthy or mindful eating as part of your lifestyle. There is a strong trend among students who traditionally sought degrees in dietetics toward more encompassing and holistic approaches like naturopathy and 'nutritional medicine' whereby they can be prescriptive with food. We need to use our food as our medicine. 'Diets' like the lemon detox diet and calorie counting diets can undermine your health especially with any fasting and fluid-type diets where you're mainly losing fluid, electrolytes and healthy gut bacteria.

Calorie counting diets make it very restrictive for a person to follow in the long term and also incorporate foods which are mainly packaged and / or not nutrient dense. People who want to detox should instead cut down on trans-fatty, highly processed foods, processed sugar, alcohol and caffeine.

MYTH No.2

Eat 3 meals a day

Only eating three meals a day usually makes one prone to snacking in between or snacking on the wrong foods anyway. That's because we are not designed to stretch out our meals. Those three meals are usually very large meals too. We are designed to eat smaller meals and more often. Usually every 2 to 3 hours. If we graze all day, we allow our metabolism to keep going. Trying to starve ourselves, skip meals or limit meals isn't good for your hormones because hormones are actually made up of fats and cholesterol. So your body needs good fats and cholesterol to function every process.

People used to think that limiting meals to three per day was good and that the body would start burning fat, but the body also eats away muscle when you starve yourself and we need muscle. Our bodies also start storing fat and glycogen levels rise after the perceived famine, just in case there is another starvation period.

So eat about six smaller meals and let your body be constantly using the food as fuel. It helps to speed your metabolism. In my experience I have also seen an overall reduction in volume consumption per day by making this small and easy change.

MYTH No.3

Salt is bad

Refined and processed salt is pervasive and added to most produced food in Western food products. People have begun to pay attention. Because salt is a natural antibiotic, it kills good bacteria in the body. As a substance that draws water, it interferes with the normal absorption of water, which possibly leads to constipation and the accumulations of toxins in the intestinal tract. Most table salts are depleted of minerals the body needs and have additives that are harmful when ingested.

On the other hand, natural salts in moderate quantities are very healthy and beneficial. Choose natural salts as a table salt replacement. The best is the Pink Peruvian salt from Power Super Foods (see the back of this book for more information on salt). Other 'good salt' alternatives are Himalayan Salt and Celtic Salt, which contain the vital minerals the body uses easily.

However, the best quality salt is the Pink Peruvian salt which is beneficial for balancing body fluids and contains the minerals the body needs without the toxins found in common table salt. It has been hand harvested for over 2000 years from a natural ancient ocean spring bubbling up to the surface in the Sacred Valley of the Incas near Machu Picchu, Peru at around 4000 metres above sea level. Pure salt sources are scarce today due to pollution of land and sea – this one is a low carbon footprint, evaporated product (not mined) and is carefully tested against heavy metal contamination.

This is the perfect healthy seasoning prized by master chefs with a deep robust flavour. The rich mineralisation, containing many trace minerals and elements, creates a lovely pale pink colour.

Benefits of ingesting natural salt are:

- It balances blood sugar and acid levels and helps the body's cells generate electrical energy.

- It acts as a natural antihistamine which regulates phlegm and mucus in the sinuses and nasal cavity.

- It helps prevent osteoporosis, muscle cramping, and irregular patterns.

- Think of it not as salt, but as minerals disguised as 'salt.' It contains so many trace minerals including calcium, iron, potassium, magnesium, copper and zinc.

You get calcium from dairy

Most of the reason we are 'moo'-ving away from cow's dairy and protein is not so much the intolerance from lactose, but more the casein intolerance. The cow is such a big animal and the protein it produces is large which makes it really hard for the human gut to digest.

The problem stems not just from the nature of the milk, but also from its production and processing. Modern feeding methods turn healthy milk products into allergens and carcinogens. This happens when high protein, soy based feeds are substituted for fresh green grass, and selective breeding creates cows with abnormally large pituitary glands so they produce three times more milk than the old fashioned cow.

On top of this genetic distortion, 50 years ago, the average cow produced 2000 pounds of milk per year, while today the top producers give 50,000 pounds. This is only possible through the wholesale administration of drugs, which then find their way into the meat, milk and all the dairy foods these creatures produce.

Due to the abnormal feeds cows are now given, they also need antibiotics to keep them well. Their milk is then pasteurised so that all valuable enzymes are destroyed. These enzymes are actually what we need to be able to digest milk, as our pancreas is not always able to produce them. Overstress of the pancreas may lead to diabetes and other lifestyle diseases.

Add to this the obsession with being skinny and the production of skinny milk. Selling skinny milk as a better milk is deceptive because the fat is there for a reason. Butterfat contains acids that have strong anti-carcinogenic properties. When it is removed by homogenisation, the milk becomes totally devoid of vitamin A, and without the butterfat, the body cannot absorb and utilise the vitamins and minerals in the remaining water fraction of the milk.

On top of this, the calcium is not even bio-available. That means we cannot assimilate it because the calcium in cows' milk is designed for a calf in the same way as the nutrition in human milk is designed for a human. So the myth that we must eat dairy to get calcium is grand. Yes, there's calcium in milk, but it's like saying there is iron in the leg of that table. Yes there is, but if you eat it, you won't get iron.

You get better sources of calcium that your body can assimilate through eating dark greens, figs, dried or fresh ones, almonds, sesame seeds and tahini. We need to be eating more of these things. Look at say Japan; they don't consume much dairy, if at all. It simply doesn't exist in their diets. Australia is one of the largest consumers of dairy in the world, yet one of the highest rates of people suffering with osteoporosis. Australians have diseases based on the lifestyle or foods eaten.

MYTH No.5

Margarine is a healthier choice

Margarine is produced by bubbling nitrogen through vegetable oil, with nickel as a catalyst. Not all the nickel is recovered so you're getting more heavy metal in your system. Even more alarming is the fact that if the producers continued the process a little longer, the margarine would turn into plastic - that's right, yummy plastic!
In fact it is one molecule away from being plastic.

We need to be careful too because there are some great companies who market their margarine packages so effectively that can trick even the smartest buyer. They seem to tick all the 'boxes'. No additives, no preservatives, non GMO, dairy free, gluten free and salt free. It is still plastic!

'As for butter versus margarine, I trust cows more than chemists.'

- Joan Gussow

Supermarket stevia and saccharin are good sugar alternatives

While we know it's important to avoid sugar, not just for our teeth, but also for our waistlines, we've been so misled into believing that artificial sweetener which has been marketed as the 'no-calorie sugar alternative', is safe. It is not. What's a dying shame is that diabetes associations have been promoting this very chemical to sufferers of diabetes. So we have started to listen and are doing great work re-educating the population on natural no-calorie alternatives such as stevia, which is safe and plant derived. You'll learn more about the above two sugar alternatives in the next chapter.

The most important thing to acknowledge is that even though stevia is natural and indeed has no calories, saccharin and aspartame companies are jumping on the no-sugar bandwagon and are marketing their products with phrases like "with the all new stevia". Once you read the information on the back of the packet, "with" is just that. Some companies add only 1% stevia and the rest is the man-made chemical, aspartame.

There are also some completely natural products on supermarket shelves that contain added malitol or eurethral to their so-called stevia. Be warned and read the backs of packets. It is mostly added because it is much cheaper to produce stevia this way. Also, by adding these substances, you won't get that bitter aftertaste, that Stevia has. Just know you're getting sugar in eurethral when you previously were thinking you weren't!

There are also some completely natural products that have malitol or eurethral added to their so-called stevia. Be warned and read the backs of your supermarket packets. It is much cheaper to produce stevia this way and by adding these substances, you won't get that bitter aftertaste when you bake with it, but you're getting sugar in eurethral and here you were thinking you weren't!

Whenever you see the words, *sugar-free, chemical-free* and *fat-free*, think *chemical storm!*

Read the backs of packets to make sure it's real food!

 Additive alerts

Artificial sweeteners

Aspartame or (E951), more popularly known as Nutrasweet and Equal, is often found in foods labelled "diet" or "sugar free". Aspartame is believed to be carcinogenic and accounts for more reports of adverse reactions than all other foods and food additives combined. Aspartame is not your friend. Aspartame is a neurotoxin and carcinogen.

Monosodium Glutamate (MSG / E621)

MSG is an amino acid used as a flavour enhancer in stocks, packaged soups, salad dressings, crisps, crackers and frozen foods. MSG is known as an excitotoxin, a substance which overexcites cells to the point of damage or death. Studies show that regular consumption of MSG may result in adverse side effects which include depression, disorientation, eye damage, fatigue, headaches, and obesity. MSG changes the neurological pathways, or nerve messages of the brain and disengage the "I'm full" function which explains the effects of weight gain. So yet another great reason to avoid this from our diet, if you're trying to keep your weight in a healthy range.

Trans fats

Trans fats are used because they are so cheap to mass produce. Manufacturers use them to enhance and extend the shelf life of products and they are among the most dangerous substances that you can consume. You will learn more about them in the chapter about fat that is about to follow. Found in deep-fried fast foods and some processed foods made with margarine or partially hydrogenated vegetable oils, canola oil and even the healthy sounding rice bran oil, they are all trans fats and are formed by a process called hydrogenation. Numerous studies show that trans fat increases LDL cholesterol levels while decreasing HDL ("good") cholesterol, increases the risk of heart attacks, heart disease and strokes, and contributes to increased inflammation, diabetes and other health problems.

Food dyes

Artificial colourings which are found in fizzy drinks, juices and many other processed foods, may contribute to behavioural problems in children.

Avoid these ones:

Blue #1 and Blue #2 (E133)
Found in lollies, cereals, soft drinks, sports drinks and pet foods. They may cause chromosomal damage and are banned in Norway, Finland and France.

Red dye #3 (also Red #40) (E124)
Banned in 1990 from use in many foods and cosmetics. It is even found in the cookies you love called 'Tim-Tams'. It has been proven to cause thyroid cancer and chromosomal damage in laboratory animals and may also interfere with brain-nerve transmission.

Dye #6 (E110) and Yellow Tartrazine (E102)
These are banned in Norway and Sweden. They increase the number of kidney and adrenal gland tumours in laboratory animals and may cause chromosomal damage.

So you see there is food dye in foods that look natural too. Who knew a chocolate colour would have red dye in it? Just because it doesn't look like a rainbow doesn't mean you're 'safe'.

Sodium sulfite (E221) is used to preserve dried fruit and meat

According to the US Food and Drug Administration (FDA),

approximately one in 100 people is sensitive to sulphites in food. The majority of these individuals are asthmatic, suggesting a link between asthma and sulfites. Individuals who are sulfite sensitive may experience headaches, breathing problems and rashes. In severe cases, sulfites can actually cause death by closing down the airway altogether, leading to cardiac arrest. Not everybody has these extreme reactions, but generally it's best to avoid these 'foods' and perhaps try drying your own. There are food dehydrators on the market that do the same thing without additives, so you can make it in the comfort of your own home.

Sulphur dioxide (E220)

Preservatives used in wine, sparkling wine and champagne are not always the best. Some people find they feel much better the next day after drinking organic wine or sparkling, because they don't contain this additive. Small amounts should be okay, however, it's best to avoid them where possible.

BHA and BHT (E320)

Butylated hydroxyanisole (BHA) and butylated hydrozyttoluene (BHT) are preservatives found in cereals, chewing gum, potato chips and vegetable oils. These common preservatives keep foods from changing colour, changing flavour or becoming rancid. BHA and BHT are oxidants which form reactive compounds in your body. They affect the neurological system of the brain, alter behaviour and have potential to cause cancer.

The best thing to do is to just not eat these foods – eat real food!

Laurentine Ten Bosch Sources: www.foodmatters.tv/articles..., www.drmercola.info, www.altmedangel.com, www.naturalnews.com and www.bestofmotherearth.com

Count chemicals, not calories

Counting calories becomes completely unnecessary when our food does not come with labels. 'Real food' is what you keep hearing. Hopefully this is starting to kick in!

Another reason to 'ditch diets' is because we need to stop calorie counting.

Start eating food that is:

- alive
- fresh
- organic
- non-processed
- full of nutrition

so that we help a part of our brain switch off the hunger mechanism. Yes, there is a part of the brain called the 'amygdala' that helps initiate the 'switching off' of the hunger mechanism. It sends a signal or message to tell you when it is full, only on a nutritional level.

So if we don't have the right type of nutrition, no matter how many or how few calories we eat, if they are not the right type, we just keep looking for 'something else'. That's why when we eat 'fast food' or junk foods that are highly processed and full of sugar and have no nutritional content, we don't stop eating. We just aren't full. We aren't full of nutrition, which is the way we are designed to eat. We are full up purely on empty calories!

We are literally overfed, undernourished and maybe even a little moody once we come down off that sugar high. We simply cannot function this way, without something giving way. The body is only adaptable for so long. We then become depleted nutritionally. So it's time we start feeding our magnificent bodies with good fuel, so that we can not only look good, but be well too.

Let's look at types of calories again. For example, some fats or foods high in good fats are higher in calories than, let's say, a glass of champagne. However, what happens to our bodies and how we process those types of calories is much more important. The fat higher in calories will be used as energy. The sugars in the alcohol help us store fat. If we are eating the right types of calories, we will be so full, we won't need other foods or calories and the right type of food we eat will also do the right thing by us too.

You *CAN* eat chocolate and ice cream

Okay, you really have read this right. It's not a misprint! Now that you know about satiation and avoiding chemicals in foods, it's easy to explain why. I'm not talking about just any chocolate or ice cream. There are certain types that don't contain additives, chemicals and addictive sugar, but do contain therapeutic good fats like cacao butter, coconut oil and low fructose, no-sugar alternatives in the ingredients like coconut nectar and rice syrup. Brands like Pana chocolate and Cocofrio ice cream you can not only eat, but they are therapeutic too. You can also make your own treats with the recipes in this book!

The reason women crave chocolate right before their menstruation is because they're in fact craving magnesium. Cacao is rich in magnesium as well as other good things like protein. Magnesium helps muscles to contract and expand well. It's found in dark leafy greens and almonds too, so having something with Cacao in it like a healthy chocolate alternative is a great way to get a 'magnesium- hit' to help you with PMS.

Your uterus is a muscle too. All organs are. So your body needs extra magnesium at that time of the month. Craving chocolate isn't bad - it's the cacao your body needs. By eating a little of that good type of chocolate without the sugar and additives, just pure cacao and coconut nectar, you're actually listening to your body and giving it what it needs to be well. Get into it!

Oh, and you can't eat too much of the good chocolate or ice cream alternative like Cocofrio. It's made from really good fats from coconut. You will feel full and your amygdala which is responsible for switching off the hunger mechanism when you are full on a nutritional level will tell you that you've had enough!

It's just that in the modern or Western world, we don't eat enough good fats because we have been programmed since the 80's to go low-fat everything! We are missing that vital nutrition. When we finally get it, we start to feel full. So if you feel like you've always been searching for something else, that something else was good fat!

This is why you won't need to count calories anymore, because you will be able to start listening to your body more when it feels full and you will literally move onto other activities.

There are too many people counting calories and not enough people counting chemicals.

Start ravaging more types of proteins and lots of them. There is protein in cacao and vegetables too, obviously not as much as meats and animal products but we must include protein with every meal. Next in line is an equally large amount of veggies.

Top plant-based protein sources are:

- quinoa
- chia seeds
- pumpkin seeds
- broccoli
- sunflower seeds
- peas
- beans
- lentils

Legumes are not considered 'Paleo', but eating 'Paleo inspired' or primal eating is better because not one diet works for all people. 'Paleo' is a term referring to the 'Hunter Gatherer' diet and times. It's also referred to as the 'caveman diet'. Lots of nuts and seeds are what we would have eaten in the Palaeolithic area. We ate all that we could pick, pluck, hunt and gather. Seeds and nuts are a great whole food as they contain good fat and protein as well as other minerals like calcium.

We then also need immune boosting fruit and fructose of the natural kind as this is actually good for us. We shouldn't avoid this. In fact, removing one whole food group from any diet is potentially dangerous. The thing that we should remove however is processed white sugar and you'll see why, now, in the next chapter!

HEY SUGAR,
WE ARE OVER

Chapter 3

"One cannot think well, love well, sleep
well, if one has not dined well."

-Virginia Woolf, A Room of One's Own

Yes, you are going to shut out the sugar and finally end this addictive relationship!

You may even discover some alternative 'loves' with which to replace your sweet habit, but I think you're 'sweet enough'!

For every molecule of sugar you consume, it takes 54 molecules of magnesium for your body to process it. Madness, right?

Even the World Health Organisation (WHO) has taken a tough stand on the sweet thing with their statement made in January 2014 recommending that sugar should account for less than 5 per cent of what people eat each day if they are to avoid health risks such as weight gain and tooth decay linked to excessively sugary diets.

This organisation is the health policy unit of the United Nations and is the largest think-tank group of people that make decisions when it comes to definitions on what health is and how to achieve it. They provide evidence-based research and recently and finally acknowledged the work of the author of *Sweet Poison*, David Gillespie who believes that sugar consumption should be severely limited. A cardiologist on the panel, Shrinath Reddy acknowledged the links between sugar and diabetes, obesity and cardiovascular disease.

For the WHO to acknowledge this philosophy makes it all the more significant.

Given that the average Australian...since the 1980s' and replace with this para: Given that sugar is hidden in so many processed foods and that the average Australian consumes around 35-45 teaspoons a day, this is a big call. Obesity in the developing world has quadrupled since the 1980's.

Something else happened in the 80's and that was the myth we were fed about 'low-fat' food. We were told to eat it and little did we know that these foods were laden with sugar! If low-fat worked, we would all be thin and we are not. It's time to say goodbye for good to low-fat and high-sugar!

Even less than a third of the population in China and India are cottoning on to this 'Western-world diet' thing, so some big rises in obesity and other sugar related diseases are forecast there too! With billions of people riding the 'chronic disease bus' the world has finally started listening to the dangers of excess sugar consumption, despite what kickbacks U.S governments are getting from the 'fast food' industry. And oh yes they do!

The main concern is how highly addictive the processed 'white stuff' is. I've been asked over and over, just how do I stay inspired? How do I stay away from the junk foods and the sugary treats? I really believe that when you understand how the body works, it will help you to understand what's happening to your body when you consume it and therefore you will be able to make better choices.

Most of the time we know something is 'bad' for us, but we still eat it. That's okay. But how do we stop eating it often? Empower yourself with the knowledge on what your body does when it consumes sugar. It will make you think twice, I promise, once you get the gist of what happens to your brain and digestion. So here we go!

Let's hear what Dr Natalie Kringoudis has to say about the sweet stuff!

"There are a host of issues sugar may cause but there are several specific ways that it affects fertility. Here is what's at the top of my list:

Sugar disrupts your hormones

Hormones are the drivers of all our body functions, but the intricacy of our sex hormones is my primary concern as a natural fertility expert. Sugar consumption will drive our insulin too high, too quickly and only momentarily. This quick peak creates a high and then we drop faster than a hot pie, leaving far more mess. This is what's known as the *fight or flight response* – the response of extended stimulation to the adrenal glands.

When our sugar levels drop, our adrenals release both cortisol and adrenalin to attempt to replenish sugar levels. Eventually this can lead to hormonal imbalance since progesterone (the main hormone required for ovulation to occur) and cortisol compete for the same receptor binding sites in the body. And cortisol is the bossy hormone – it will always win over progesterone. Should this continue for a period of time, the entire endocrine system will be upset and will lead to disruption of all sex hormones - oestrogen, progesterone, the androgens DHEA and testosterone for both sexes.

Sugar is inflammatory

Inflammation is simply our body's response to damage, be it from infection, illness or allergies. Sugar is inflammatory, mostly because our bodies aren't designed to consume the quantities we see in modern Western diets and our gut goes into a frenzy trying to cope. Inflammation is a normal body response toward recovery. This is especially appropriate for women who suffer from endometriosis. Most women who cut sugar out of their diet will notice substantial changes and in some instances total recovery from endometriosis. When it comes to fertility and conception, endometriosis can be an issue as it affects the uterine lining and making implantation of the embryo difficult.

Sugar leads to insulin resistance

Insulin is released by the pancreas to convert sugar to energy. However, the more sugar we eat, the more insulin the pancreas releases, eventually leading to insulin resistance. Insulin resistance can be to blame for issues with ovulation, maturation of the egg and implantation of the embryo into the uterine lining. What's more, these women are at a far higher risk of miscarriage than the average. Many women who have polycystic ovary syndrome (PCOS) have insulin resistance.

Sugar consumption can make PMS worse

Not only because of the inflammation already spoken of but also because of the hormone disruption also mentioned – and let's not forget, fertility isn't just about the babies! Feeling well all month round is part of having healthy, happy hormones.

Sugar zaps your vitamin and mineral stores

This can be a massive fertility factor. Our hormones require specific amounts of vitamins and minerals to be well-fuelled. The pill severely depletes our vitamin and mineral stores, as does fructose. When our stores are low, our entire body is compromised, which contributes to amenorrhea, irregular periods, lower immunity, increased infection (which can be a factor in miscarriage too), increased anxiety, depression, irritable bowel syndrome and the list goes on. Very often, the end 'diagnosis' is unexplained infertility. Because of this, it also ages us. Cutting out sugar could have you looking younger, sooner than you may think.

Rather than reaching for another pack of biscuits as you digest this information, perhaps think about how you can begin to lessen sugar in your diet. Our bodies aren't designed to tolerate much sugar especially of the refined, processed variety. But also for many women, high sugar natural foods like fruits can too be troublesome.

Most of all, I encourage you to figure out what works best for you – experiment with the idea of quitting sugar. I bet you'll be pleasantly surprised, period pain free and looking younger in no time.

When you consume sugar you suddenly raise your balanced ratios past their ideal levels. This can cause the adrenals to become active and gets the liver active to try and store these excessive sugars as glycogen. But like a sponge, there is only so much that the liver can store and only so long it can keep working before it is exhausted. What I've described can lead to 'the sugar hit' we have all had and then the crash when the adrenals are exhausted, which is very unhealthy and also toxic."

So it's actually not good fat that makes you fat. Sugar makes you fat! Low calorie foods may well be low in just that - the calories, but it's the type of calories that are more important to us. If the food is high in sugar and low in nutrition and good fat, you will put on weight. You can read more about this in the next chapter which is all about fat!

Get your body to use sugar so that you don't store it

You've got to get your body to use sugar straight away if you don't want it to be stored as fat. This seems pretty simple to do, but why aren't we doing it then? It's because we are not eating REAL sugar. This is where we need to focus once again on eating REAL FOOD. The white processed sugar, or even raw sugar, has been processed and the body doesn't recognise it as REAL FIT FOOD.

So Dr Damian Kristof who has the know-how on nutrition and chiropractic, understands how the digestive system and nervous system (brain, spinal cord and nerves) work together to make this happen. He explains it this way: when sugar goes into the blood stream, the blood sugar levels increase. The brain registers this increase in glucose and sends a signal down the spinal cord to the pancreas. The pancreas recognises that message and sends out insulin. This process assists with the uptake of sugar, in combination with thyroid hormones.

Cells within the body that require sugar, but don't need insulin, like the brain for example (and yes your body does require sugar), are already taking up sugar and will be using sugar straight away! However this sugar has to be in the simplest form. This is glucose which can come from fructose in fruit or lactose, sucrose, galactose and all different types of sugars. These get broken down to become the glucose. The body has to be using it at a certain speed though, or it becomes toxic by storing it. The brain then malfunctions. This is what happens when we have diabetes or obesity for example. It's when our body stores sugar because we are not using it straight away.

In a nutshell, when you eat any kind of sugar, the brain registers that there is an increase in blood sugar and sends a message out to the pancreas to secrete insulin and insulin helps the body use sugar. If it's not used immediately, it will start to store it.

Now everybody has hormones that help us have an 'on-off' switch through our genes that help us understand when we are satiated so we can stop eating when we are nutritionally satisfied. There are only a handful of us that do not get that message - about 5% of the population have that genetic defect.

However, if a food source becomes more and more highly processed, the less information is attached to that food product. Dr Damian uses the term 'information' to define the amount of nutrition in that food. There are *macro-nutrients*, which are proteins, fats and carbohydrates and *micro-nutrients*, which are the vitamins and minerals that come from that food source. Vitamins and minerals are the information that satiate the brain. These nutrients get stripped away, the more something becomes processed.

Here's an example with the star of this chapter, sugar! Sugar comes from sugar cane. This is a whole food in its entirety. It's raw, whole and unprocessed. If we chewed this cane, it would be a little sweet but not too sweet. It also has other nutrition in it, because it is a whole food, for example fibre. If we had to take the juice out, it would be sweeter. If we then dried the juice out of it, it would be sweeter again, because we took the water out of it, which would have diluted it. If we continued the 'process', hence the term 'processed sugar, we would get raw sugar, then white sugar, then castor sugar, then icing sugar as it becomes finer and sweeter and more highly processed.

If it is heated, we burn off all the nutrition. It's not longer a real food or a whole food. It is now highly processed, the form has been concentrated and as a result it has lost its micro-nutrients which is what we need to keep us full. All the nutrition has now been lost. Had we chewed on the sugar cane, we would have had more satiation and would have felt fuller quicker. There is no off-switch working in our brains anymore when we eat processed food, because there's no 'information' (aka micro-nutrition) to help us feel full and satiated.

Another example are the juices you may buy for your kids. These juices often contain only 5% fruit juice; the rest is sugar. There may be the same amount of 'calories' as a full freshly squeezed orange juice, but because there's only 5% nutrition, the brain doesn't get any information from the intelligence in the food that was normally there when it was a whole food in its entirety. That's why the kids just can't get enough and are still hungry and possibly moody. They have missed out on what their brains need. We, as adults, are no different.

So the more real and whole the food is, the more you help your brain and body to work better and the more you do this, the fuller you will feel. So ditch the processed sugar and eat more sugars from other sources, because we need them too.

We need sugar from fruits. The only reason we may be intolerant to things like fructose or lactose is because our digestive system is no longer working well and cannot naturally use the sugar. Real sugar from fruit is mixed with other vital micro-nutrients like potassium or vitamin C. If we have trouble with digestion of the fructose or lactose, which is what can be known as IBS or irritable bowel syndrome, it can be from the gut not working well from stress or from overuse of medications.

This is where we lose the natural flora and fauna in the gut. So this is why it's great to work with natural healthcare practitioners like wellness chiropractors, naturopaths, Chinese medicine doctors and nutritionists, who are interested in restoring gut and nerve system health. When that part of you works well, you are well. And here's the answer: you can use sugar, not store sugar.

No-sugar, man-made foods are just as dangerous. They are usually the ones made with chemicals like aspartame. So far from our roots, and even more distant to being natural, is this very notion that if we eat artificially sweetened foods then we will also lose weight. We were oh so wrong.

Below is an extract from *7 Things Your Doctor Forgot to Tell You*.

MYTH

Artificial sweetener helps you lose weight

Artificial sweetener has been promoted as the great breakthrough for weight watchers because it is virtually calorie free. It's actually misleading. Even though it has no calories, it is a chemical that your body doesn't know how to digest, and by making it harder to process foods actually slows down your digestive system, thereby causing weight gain. As unwelcome as that is, it is actually benign compared to its many other side effects.

Most foods that are labelled 'low fat' or 'light' will contain artificial sweetener, and again you may think you're losing weight or being healthier by eating less sugar or fat, but these chemicals slow down the digestive system and may actually make you put on weight. Argh!

The effects go beyond this, because studies show that long-term use creates an environment for blood-borne cancers like lymphoma to develop. All this time we have been led to believe that we were making healthier choices when we opted for artificial sweeteners, just because they had fewer calories.

You're now getting an inkling of the possible dangers of regular aspartame consumption. There are countless reports from doctors and nutritionists who have 'cured' their clients of many conditions, simply by removing aspartame from their diets.

The multi-billion dollar aspartame industry would have us believe that "aspartame kills" is an urban legend, and that it would require the consumption of 100 cans of diet soda a day to be harmed by their product. Despite it being untrue, their main claim is that the three components of aspartame are found in many natural foods and are therefore safe. This is like saying that carbon monoxide is safe because it contains only carbon and oxygen, the same components as carbon dioxide.

The following report by Felicity Lawrence further explores the controversy surrounding man-made artificial sweeteners.

50

Methanol (wood alcohol) makes up 10% of aspartame and is highly toxic — the minimum lethal dose for an adult is two teaspoons. It is also found in some fruits and vegetables, but never occurs in natural foods without ethanol and pectin, its 'antidotes'. Ethanol & pectin prevent methanol from being metabolised into formaldehyde (embalming fluid) & formic acid (the same chemical as fire ant venom), both deadly toxins. An ethanol drip is the standard emergency room treatment for methanol poisoning. Aspartame contains no ethanol or pectin; therefore the methanol is converted to formaldehyde and formic acid in your body when you consume it, which are toxic.

The sickly sweet facts

Aspartame, the essential ingredient in many artificial sweeteners, breaks down to phenylalanine, aspartic acid, and methanol when heated, and also within our warm bodies. The methanol is further metabolised into formaldehyde, a poison known to damage the immune and nervous system as well as cause genetic damage.

Aspartame breaks down the protective coating surrounding neurons in our brain, causing a break in the blood-brain barrier and allowing toxins to move directly into the bloodstream, with a whole cascade of destructive effects.

About 10% of the population has a tendency to multiple sclerosis (MS) but never actually develop the symptoms, and these people can be pushed into full-blown MS with continual usage of products containing aspartame.

Almost half of aspartame by weight is itself a toxin, technically an excitotoxin (a substance that damages nerve cells). Research done on 1800 rats showed that it causes cancer of the kidney and of the peripheral nerves in the head. Earlier data from the same study linked aspartame to a greater risk of leukaemia and lymphomas, even at doses very close to what is considered the acceptable daily intake for humans. Obviously, with such a list of dangerous side effects, aspartame should never be given to children.

The study concluded that consuming products containing aspartame may contribute to ailments such as birth defects, brain cancer, chronic fatigue, diabetes, dizziness, emotional disorders, epilepsy, Graves' disease, headaches, lowered sperm count, migraines, multiple sclerosis (MS) and Parkinson's disease symptoms.

We know about how artificial sweetener is bad now. The other leading artificial sweetener is saccharin, which is popular because it is so much sweeter than sugar. It has been in use for longer than any other artificial sweetener, and has been subjected to the most studies. When research linked it to cancer in 1977, it was not banned because there were no alternative sweeteners for diabetics at the time. The U.S. permitted its use as long as manufacturers affixed a warning label, so in that country many products like chewing gum bear the legend: *"This product contains saccharin, which has been known to cause cancer in laboratory animals"*. Hopefully we will have the same warning labels on our foods in the rest of the world, to alert us to the dangers of the consumption.

Cyclamate was also at one time a widely used artificial sweetener, but this chemical has been banned in the U.S. since 1970 based on its possible link with cancer.

Dr Joseph Mercola (www.mercola.com) has dedicated his life to revealing the truth behind artificial sweeteners, and has published the results of his research in the book, *Sweet Deception*. This topic deserves a whole book on its own, so if you really want to know the facts this is an excellent source. It will shake any blind trust you might have in the authorities overseeing what is allowed to be added and done to our food, and give you a fuller understanding of just how decisions by organisations like the U.S. Food And Drug Administration (FDA) may be hazardous to your health. In 1970, former FDA commissioner Charles Edwards said:

"People think the FDA is protecting them. It isn't. What the FDA is doing and what the people think it's doing are different as night and day."

San Francisco Chronicle, 2 January 1970

In that instance he was referring to the fact that the FDA not only works to protect 'pharma-business', but also actively works against good health practices and has done so for years.

Note: If you are diabetic, then you have good reason to seek alternate sweet sources, but choose wisely. There are many natural sweeteners that are much safer than any artificial ones, and once you reduce your sweets consumption, it is likely that your cravings will also abate.

There are alternatives

Stevia and Xylitol vs. sugar and artificial sweetener

Stevia is made from the leaves of the South American plant *stevia rebaudiana*. As a herb and a natural sweetener it is superior to any artificial product. Sweeter than regular sugar and with far fewer calories, it is used to sweeten tea in Japan and South America. Stevia is beneficial in balancing blood sugar, and has antimicrobial properties.

53

Again, moderation is the key, but when such excellent herbal alternatives are available you needn't sweeten anything artificially.

Xylitol (dextrose) is another alternative to sugar and artificial sweeteners, and may be used safely in small amounts. Derived from the birch tree, it is widely used in chewing gums as it inhibits bacterial growth and reduces the incidence of cavities. It tastes exactly like sugar, and is especially good for diabetics and those who are hypoglycaemic. A 1986 study verified Xylitol's safety — it received the highest and safest ADI (acceptable daily intake) rating. You can purchase xylitol from health food stores and use it as a sweetener in drinks and baked goods.

It's a great sugar alternative and has 40% less calories than sugar. It's also plant-derived, which means it's natural, unlike aspartame, which has been known to be carcinogenic and affect the digestive system.

Agave nectar is also plant-derived and a great sugar alternative. The texture is more like syrup than thick honey. It makes it a great consistency for baking. There are 'lighter' versions of agave nectar, but the light type means it is only lighter in colour, not calories, so choose the darker amber colour, which has a rich, delicious flavour.

While no sweetener is without controversy, artificial sweeteners can be quite damaging to our health and may cause serious illness (as I discussed in the previous chapter). If you have the choice, and you do, it's best to avoid them completely. Some people choose them because they've been led to believe that artificial sweetener is actually healthier and better for them than sugar. It is not. All artificial sweeteners are exactly that — artificial.

So you're already doing all the right things and exercising, right?

What's wrong then? Well the key to unlock 'thin' is to avoid sugar, eat good fats often, allow better nutritional value through eating organic and make sure your body can assimilate the great nutrition.

FATS AND FACTS
Chapter 4

"To eat is a necessity, but to eat intelligently is an art."

- La Rochefoucauld

Types of Fats

The type of fat you eat can mean the difference between fuel-up and blow-out. This chapter is an excerpt from *Eat Fat, Be Thin*, co-authored with Dr Natalie Kringoudis, and will reveal information about different types of fat that will empower you to make conscious, healthy living choices that will set you and your family up for long and happy lives free from the burden of weight watching. The bonus is that when you learn about types of fats and how to use them, you will achieve not only a better figure, but better health too.

Eating healthily no longer has to be boring. If you're going to eat, you may as well eat food that is guilt free and has maximum taste. The added bonus is that it is nutritious. And you're about to find out how eating our recommended fats and cakes, combined with a healthy and active lifestyle, can actually keep you thin.

Here's the 'low-down' on 'low-fat'. The new 'black' is 'high-fat'. You read it right! Low fat is a thing of the past. High fat is actually how we are designed to eat. Quality therapeutic fats will never make us fat.

There are four main types of fat - saturated, polyunsaturated, monounsaturated and trans fats. We need the first three in our diets, but because some are better for us than others. It's also important to become aware of the amounts of which fats you are eating. But ditch those trans fats!

Some fats are healthier to cook with than others. Let's look at each of the fats in turn.

 FAT TYPE #1

Saturated Fats

Butter, lard, cream, other dairy, meat, poultry with skin on, cheese, fried foods.

These foods also contain dietary cholesterol. Many baked goods and fried foods can contain high levels of saturated fats. Some plant foods, such as palm oil, palm kernel oil and coconut oil also contain primarily saturated fats, but do not contain cholesterol.

Saturated fats fall into two categories:

1. those that are high in saturated fatty acids (and therefore lower in unsaturated fatty acids), and
2. those that are lower in saturated fatty acids (but are higher in unsaturated fatty acids).

The latter is much better for you and, as you will discover, many of our recipes contain plant foods that offer saturated fats like coconut butter (or coconut oil – they are the same thing).

We need to be cautious with these kinds of fats. Foods high in the saturated kind have been linked to cardiovascular disease and cancer, and for this reason, it's important to be mindful of how much of this type of fat you are consuming, specifically saturated fats from meats, dairy and poultry.

Fats from plants are an entirely different story. The benefits of the saturated fats from plants are vast; because of their therapeutic qualities they are key when it comes to eating fat and still being thin.

Coconut oil gets our seal of approval. It's just so versatile. Some oils become carcinogenic (cancer-causing) when heated at high temperatures, but not coconut oil. Look for cold-pressed organic coconut oil, which is exactly that – cold-pressed when it's extracted from the coconut. It's solidified, which means it makes a good butter alternative too.

Being able to cook with it at high temperatures is not the only great thing about coconut oil either. The properties in coconut oil are comparable to colostrum, since both coconut oil and mother's milk contain medium chain fatty acids that nourish, are easily absorbed and protect the body against illness.

The essential fatty acids are just that: essential. As part of healthy fats, they have a key role in maximising health. Consuming them means you can have fewer cravings and greater satisfaction because you feel fuller, and they help you burn more calories by increasing energy and metabolism – all this just by eating healthy fats! Here lies the big bonus: they may actually help you lose weight.

These reasons are why you'll see coconut oil in many of our recipes. In fact, using coconut in any form is extremely healthy for you. Try using shredded coconut. It's another 'super fat' and also super tasty in cakes and treats.

FAT TYPE #2

Polyunsaturated Fats

Vegetable oils including soybean oil, corn oil and safflower oil, as well as fatty fish such as salmon, mackerel, herring and trout. Other sources include some nuts and seeds such as walnuts and sunflower seeds.

Omega 3 and Omega 6 are found in many foods high in polyunsaturated fats (think oily fish, nuts and seeds), and are your friends for cardiovascular health. These are key fats to include in your diet and are especially vital for the expecting mother who will need this type of nutrition for both her and her growing new baby. It's awesome brain food!

Omega 3 fatty acids are essential for healthy foetal development, but they are also wonderful for healthy skin, good vision and overall wellness, right down to treating mood disorders and moving post-baby weight.

As well as being an excellent way of getting essential fatty acids, nuts and seeds are also an excellent source of protein for vegans and vegetarians.

FAT TYPE #3

Monounsaturated Fats

Vegetable oils such as olive oil, canola oil, peanut oil, sunflower oil and sesame oil. Other sources include avocados, peanut butter, and many nuts and seeds.

Related to these three main types of fat are trans fats. Trans fats are unsaturated fats (mostly from plants) that have been hydrogenated, which means they have had hydrogen added to them. This process usually happens in food processing, particularly in the production of hard margarines. And we now know just how bad it is to eat margarine now.

There are other ways to lower cholesterol. There is increasing evidence that trans fats are probably the worst of all fats for our health.

Even more shocking news is that margarine is one molecule away from being plastic. Stick it outside in direct sunshine and it fails to melt. And we eat this? Even more shocking is the notion that eating specific margarines is the means to lower cholesterol.

We are not advocates of eating near plastic to lower cholesterol. There is increasing evidence that trans fats are probably the worst of all fats for our health.

But it's not all bad news when it comes to monosaturated fats. Avocados (which also contain polyunsaturated fat) are an amazing source of monosaturated fat and provide an outstanding nutritional advantage, especially when it comes to weight loss and hormone function.

Get avocados into your system any way you can: put them in salads or a salsa dip, on rye crackers with a slice of a favourite vegetable, or eat with a spoon and some cracked pepper and sea salt.

Avocados target the health and function of the womb and cervix of the female – they even look just like these organs, with the shape replicating the womb, and the seed, the baby. When a woman eats one avocado a week, it balances hormones, sheds unwanted birth weight, and helps prevent cervical cancers. And how profound is this fact? It takes exactly nine months to grow an avocado from blossom to ripened fruit.

FAT TYPE #4

Trans Fats

Trans fats can be found in many foods like margarine, but especially in fried foods like French fries and doughnuts, in baked goods including pastries, pie crusts, biscuits, pizza dough, cookies, crackers, and in all margarines and shortenings. You can determine the amount of trans fats in a particular packaged food by looking at the nutritional panel on the side of the package.

The most important thing to get from this is **DO NOT EAT** trans fats. They have been chemically altered and because of this, offer very little nutritional benefit. Basically, anything that is too processed or altered from its natural state is not really 'food' anymore.

Try to eat things that are as close to nature as possible. Trans fats are much more harmful to body function than saturated fats, and therefore should be avoided.

However do not fret, because you can still have your cake and it eat it too! This book has a variety of tasty recipes that do not use any trans fats. You will not miss out and can still eat everything from torte to tart and cupcake to cake. Next time you get invited to someone's house for dinner or tea and cake, you may like to bring your own 'healthy' version you learned to make from this book and spread the love around.

Some of these oils do a have a place in your pantry. Olive, peanut, quality sunflower and sesame oil can be great for pouring, meaning they will not only make your salad or dish taste delicious, but will make it nutritious too. Canola oil is best avoided as it is genetically engineered and doesn't tick any 'health favour' boxes for this reason.

Why is fat good for you?

Fat has been the big, bad wolf when it comes to being and looking thin and fit. Health-conscious people across the globe are buying 'low fat', 'light' and fewer-calorie options when it comes to food. "Oh, don't touch that cake!" and "A moment on the lips, a lifetime on the hips" are phrases we have all heard before. However, somewhere along the line we tipped the scales, grabbed the life jackets and headed for a sinking boat, despite our best efforts to stay thin and be healthy.

The truth is that fat is actually good for you. And that's not all. It also helps you to lose weight when you eat the right type.

The health benefits of eating the right fats are many. They are essential for nervous system function and brain development, hence the term Essential Fatty Acids (EFAs). We all need these types of fat in our diet. Without them we would miss out on vital nutrients — vitamins A, D and E that are needed to prevent or control all kinds of symptoms and conditions such as heart disease, cancers, immune system deficiencies, arthritis, skin complaints, PMS and menopausal symptoms. They are also critical for a healthy reproductive function, as hormones are made of fats and proteins.

Is it any wonder then why we are seeing women's health problems on the rise at the same time women's hips are growing? The scales have been tipped way too far in the wrong direction.

Low fat foods have been linked to infertility in both men and women. As we discussed earlier, this is because they don't contain the adequate nutrients that their full-fat siblings provide. Whole foods are always, hands down, the best option. And there are extra benefits. You can end up with a stronger immune system or become more fertile.

Fats are also a great source of energy and because they don't store water, they can be used to store almost twice the amount of energy compared to protein or carbohydrate.

Fats have huge benefits. So there's nothing to be afraid of, or send you running to the treadmill. Take a deep yoga breath and relax knowing that the best news of all is: fats make us full; they help us to be satisfied so we don't overeat. Genius!

So when did we get so scared of fat?

In a nutshell, fat was blamed for heart disease. American scientist Ancel Keys observed that people who had a diet high in fat were more likely to develop heart disease, so he went on a crusade encouraging people to cut the fat. His logic was that when you ate fat, this same fat transferred to your heart, arteries and around your organs.

But most of the cultures he observed had the same Western way of eating. Had he gathered information using several more cultural groups like the Greeks or Inuits, he would have found that some cultures have a diet high in fat yet have low rates of heart disease.

We also need to learn that cholesterol is actually good. We can help ourselves by eating good cholesterol. And you thought that we had to steer clear of it because it too was a no-no?

You'll be pleased to know that:

- our hormones are made of cholesterol – especially our sex hormones.
- the fat we have circulating in our system is saturated (saturated or monounsaturated fat) since we are essentially animals and this is a vital life ingredient that we make ourselves or get from our food (but not necessarily from saturated fat).
- eggs are good fats. But know this: free-range eggs/ organic eggs contain 50% more omega oils than battery range eggs.

Throw away the old notion that too many eggs are bad for you. Since we can regularly eat eggs, it seems there isn't necessarily 'good' and 'bad' cholesterol, but rather just cholesterol.

To cut a very long story short, the types of food we eat will contribute to the levels of cholesterol present in the body. The higher amount of cholesterol present, the more danger it poses to your health. But remember, we do need some cholesterol in our bodies – at least enough to make our hormones.

Saturated and trans fats influence cholesterol the most. What research has now found is that a diet low in fat can potentially shoot your cholesterol levels through the roof. On top of this, most low fat foods you encounter are full of fructose, which is the type of sugar that makes us fat. So the combination of a food being low fat and also lacking nutritional value is disastrous.

So how much fat can you have? Good question. This is tricky to answer since we aren't all built the same. Most of the recipes you will find in this book combine fat and protein, which is a darn good mix, not just for your taste buds; it also makes your health go gangbusters.

So, does this mean we should eat less saturated fat since it increases cholesterol? That really depends on what you replace it with. You now know that if you were to replace saturated fat with low-fat options or hydrogenated products you'd be gearing up to jump up a few dress sizes and cause some terrible strain on your innards. But if you replaced the saturated fats with polyunsaturated fats, you'd be doing yourself, your heart and your buttocks a favour.

The thing is, your body can't make monounsaturated and polyunsaturated fats. It must get them from dietary sources, so it is essential to pump up the intake to move toward better health. The best combo is less saturated fats and more of the polyunsaturated and monounsaturated varieties.

So there is nothing wrong with eating an egg a day. In fact, you could have seven. They are a perfect food and provide all the nutrients we need. You could probably survive on a diet of eggs. And lots of our cakes use eggs so hooray for our hormones, health and happiness.

So how much of the good stuff can we have?

As a rule, to maintain great health and good nutrition, we need a rough mix of all three – protein, low GI carbohydrates and therapeutic fats. Roughly 20-30% of this should be made up of these therapeutic fats.

However, the mix of fats that you eat, rather than the total amount in your diet, is what matters most when it comes to your cholesterol and health. The key is to eat more good fats and less bad fats. Isn't it great that we are now including cholesterol in this list? So a perfect example of a daily intake of fats may be:

Breakfast
Eggs and half an avocado with a vegetable. Eat the eggs whatever way you like them. They are a complete meal. Fry them with lots of coconut oil.

Snack
Let them eat cake! Any recipe from *Eat Fat Be Thin* is a winner (go to the snack section for ideas) or the Amazeballs from this book!

Lunch
Moroccan chicken and a coleslaw salad with mayonnaise or tahini.

Snack
Veggie sticks with hummus or a coconut milk smoothie with coconut oil.

Dinner
Salmon steak and salad with good cold-pressed organic nut oil.

A clever diet

The best way to fuel your body is to eat foods that are as close to nature as possible. The more alive your foods are, the more life they will have and therefore give you. So make fresh fruits and vegetables your main source, and include protein in every meal. Muscles need protein to grow and women in general don't eat enough. It does not need to be meat. You can get protein sources from boiled eggs, nuts (which contain fats — extra bonus!), goat's cheese, quinoa and legumes.

Eating fats in all meals means knowing which are good to eat, and which you need to ditch.

Eat up

With saturated fats, good fats for hot uses are coconut and palm oils, biodynamic butter, eggs, meat and seafood. Good unsaturated fats for cold uses are olive oil, sesame, nut, flaxseed, avocado and chia seed oils.

Cacao butter is great as it has a neutral effect on blood triglyceride (fat) levels. Most cacao butter in Australia is cosmetic grade and can be extracted with heat or solvents and have chemical residues. It's really important that people don't cheap out! There is more information here if you need it: *http://www.powersuperfoods.com.au/cacao/cacao-butter. html#tab_nf*

DITCH saturated fats

like margarine, hydrogenated oils or even partly hydrogenated oils and oil-blend margarines. Say bye-bye to these unsaturated bad guys too: canola, corn, vegetable, soybean, grapeseed, sunflower, safflower and rice bran oils. They're all highly processed.

Add that to the fact that you could get some of that intake by eating from one of our recipes and you will think this new diet is literally a 'piece of cake'.

Notice something is missing? Yes, that's flour and bread. The ingredients to use in the cakes should not contain wheat. Use flours that don't contain gluten, including coconut flour, rice flour, millet flour, quinoa flour, amaranth flour and sometimes spelt flour. Spelt contains gluten but is a very easily digested grain and doesn't upset the stomach unlike its sibling, whole-wheat flour.

If you are gluten intolerant, recipes like Amazeballs with puffed amaranth instead of rolled oats are perfect for you. The almond meal and coconut flours are gluten free, very nutritious and high in essential fatty acids and protein. Forage, which is the company that nutritionist Dr Damian Kristof developed, has a great range of cereals too that are wheat and gluten free and they taste delicious.

Wheat contains gluten, which is a protein that is really difficult to digest and has been linked with a host of health problems including depression, migraines and cancer among others. When we eat it, our gut goes into inflammation frenzy as it tries to digest it, and over time our adrenals become exhausted with this constant reaction to the inflammation in the intestines. The result can be a very sick, tired and fat body.

Yes, wheat can make you fat because it is converted to sugar and also because eventually the adrenals have no capacity left to produce necessary hormones to digest. Perhaps this reaction may not have been as bad, had we not genetically modified wheat it so that it grew better, faster and was more resilient to bugs and droughts.

As you can see, there's no end to eating fat. It's the wheat and sugar-converted fat that sits on your body that is the enemy. The real fat oils slide through your system, making your body run like a well-oiled engine. Go enjoy it all day and every day as long as it's the right stuff.

So, remember good fats don't make you fat. Sugar does. Good fats are called E.F.A's or Essential Fatty Acids for a reason – they are crucial to consume if you want overall good health.

"Those who think they have no time for exercise will sooner or later have to find time for illness."
- Edward Stanley

Okay, so you don't have time to train.

I get it. I sure do! I mean, who does? We have an abundance of bills to pay, washing to do, kids to attend to and partners to please. How do you fit in gym? It's called training intelligence. You need to start exercising smart. This means shorter bursts of more intense varied exercise!

We're all guilty. Before we knew any better, we exercised like fools with countless hours of running on the treadmill and the same workout regime, week after week. The most ironic part of the story is that there were little results. We still struggled to keep the weight off because we were misinformed and on the low-fat bandwagon.

What a breath of fresh air it is to grasp the concept of eating for wellness and health: eating fat and exercising right. Who knew it could be this easy? So you get to combine the two and you're set!

The first thing you need to create is an understanding of how important it is to make the time and then next, you will need to follow these rules for creating incidental exercise. Another way is to exercise smart and hard.

Time-poor fit tips

Training smart or intelligently means you throw away the old belief system that training must take an hour or hour and a half and that it has to only be in a gym.

While exercising with others is awesome for motivation and inspiration as well as keeping you committed to a person or trainer to make sure you front up, you also may have the best training partner, right at home - your child!

Okay, so your baby toddler wants to play or be held. Wonderful news! Wear your baby! It's the best training accessory! Your new dumbbell is your Velcro child. Let's say baby is teething or tired and just wants to be close. This is a good thing. Baby wearing is an instinctive parenting style that allows you to keep them close in a sling, wrap or punch for a part of the day. It gives you the freedom to go about daily activity while attending to your child's developmental needs.

You see, wearing your baby allows them to be AT the centre of activity, not THE centre of attention, which is a wonderful environment proven to stimulate brain development and cognitive learning.

Social conditioning has previously led parents to believe that if a baby is held frequently, they will grow up spoilt, clingy or demanding. Modern research reveals quite the opposite. The physical and psychological benefits of baby-wearing encourages children to feel secure and content while the rational part of their brain is still integrating with the mammalian and reptilian parts. It builds a solid sense of self esteem. The closeness helps parents to get to know baby's needs before they start fussing too, which means less crying for all parties involved.

Wearing your baby means baby is rocked and moved too. This is crucial for neurological development where the vestibular part of the brain requires rocking and motion for development. That's why when someone hands you a baby, you instinctively start rocking.

I've seen a mother in a supermarket with baby on the hip and she was rocking the shopping trolley backwards and forwards. Hilarious! There's proof!

So start exercising with your child and if you don't have one, find a friend who does. I'm sure they'd be more than grateful if you offered to take them for an hour while they caught up on chores and sleep!

How to train with small people

- wear your child and walk up hills or stairs. Make sure you get a really good baby carrier that is good for your and your child's spines. The best is the Ergo baby. It has been approved by chiropractors and can take the weight of up to a four year old if you're hiking.

- use the child for forms of play like the aeroplane ride. This is great for legs and abs.

- allow an older child to climb on your back and do push-ups from the feet or knees.

- wear or cuddle the child tightly and squat. See following chapter on how to squat properly.

You may also get creative and think of some other exercises too. Children make great weights.

Train insane or remain the same

We all need it, but exercising right is key – and not exercising with the main focus being to lose weight. Exercising to be healthy is right on the money. Exercise is vital for every part of us – the physical and the mental – as it aids in hormone regulation. It is the best way to move cortisol (the stress hormone) out of your body, and the endorphins that are released after a workout are equally as good as eating treats from this book.

My Crossfit Coach and BJJ martial artist, Gavin Ward agrees that constant, varied exercise is the best form of exercise. Think about how bored you'd get eating the same meal for breakfast, lunch and dinner day after day, or watching the same TV episode over and over. Your muscles are no different. Doing the same workout week in, week out, is not only a waste of your time, but your muscles' time too. It's as though they've gone to sleep mid-workout because they're running on autopilot. Muscles needed to be constantly shocked by new stimulus pushing them to move, grow and adapt to different situations.

Unless you're training to be a body builder steer clear of the isolation exercises at the gym like the leg curl/extension machines and doing set after set of bicep curls. As good as your arms will look in a singlet, being able to bicep curl a 45kg dumbbell for ten reps has very little carry over in your daily life. Instead, ditch the dumbbell and hit the pull up bar. You'll still get a great bicep workout but will also include muscle groups in your back, shoulders, arms and abdominal and even pelvic floor.

Forget the old notion that you need to train for over an hour each time you step into the gym for a workout. Instead focus on doing a more intense workout for a shorter period of time. A high intensity workout where you focus on using functional movements will work more muscle groups per exercise giving you a better overall workout and save you time.

So now we are talking intelligent training!

When you see fit people, yes they work hard at what they do, but they're just as busy as anyone else. Here are the differences:

1.   They are committed and have made a choice to make it part of their lifestyle

and here's the important part:

2.   They are doing types of movements and exercises that get better results.

There are some types of exercises you can do that are more supreme to others. These movements and exercises are also the way your body is designed to move, so they're actually healthier and better for you.

The below exercises may look or sound difficult to you initially, but they are natural movements and are safe and effective because you're activating more muscle groups, which is better for you and your core.

These exercises are called 'Functional Movements'.

Here are our favourites:

 Deadlifts

Sounds scary, right? In fact, the name is silly because a deadlift is one of the most functional movements you can perform. The name actually refers to lifting a dead weight from the ground, whether it is actual weights, groceries or even a child. Everyone performs dozens of deadlifts everyday without thinking twice. A strong back is crucial to every individual, regardless of age, and this is exactly one of the muscle groups it works!

Your entire posterior chain (back and glutes - better understood as butt cheeks and hamstrings), quadriceps, abs and obliques of the trunk, not to mention the grip strength required by the forearms are all getting a workout in this one exercise!

But you really have to get the movement right. Whether you are attempting deadlifts for the first time with very small weights or just a barbell with no weights at all and are no stranger to the movement, you will need to take heed of these pointers below. This will not only ensure that you minimise the risk of injury, but will see greater results with time.

Take a grip on the bar 2-3 fingers wider than your hips.

Your feet should be no wider that shoulder width.

Keep your arms straight, weight in your heels, not toes and flare your knees outwards toward your forearms to activate your glutes.

Make sure your back is straight and abs are tight and activated throughout the movement.

Now one of the most important parts of the exercise is the breathing.

Take a big breath in and hold it in throughout the movement. Make sure your head stays neutral with your body, that means ears in line with the shoulders and keep the bar as close to you as possible during the lift.

Lift from your chest.

If your butt lifts first you'll lock out your knees too early and put the entire load on your lower back. As the bar passes your knees thrust forward with your hips and squeeze your butt cheeks (yes I said squeeze) to lock out your hips (and knees). Knees and hips need to lock out simultaneously forming a straight line between your feet, knees and hips.

Focus on all that technique before you even think about adding any weight to a bar! You will still be getting a great workout.

Squats

There are many variations of squats: front squats, high bar back squats, low bar back squats and air squats. Let's assume in this instance we are doing a back squat (barbell positioned on your trapezius muscles - across shoulders).

Depending on your level of mobility, you can play around with the width of your stance but you need to be standing approximately shoulder width with the toes slightly turned out.

Keep the weight in your heels. There is no power in your toes here. Keep chest up, and shoulders back with a slight arch in your back, head looking forward or slightly up to keep correct spinal alignment.

Correct breathing is key with any lift.

Take a big breath in before you lower yourself down into the squat and only breathe out once you've returned back to a standing position.

If you breathe out on the way up under tension (a weighted barbell) you'll lose midline stability, have a weaker trunk and potentially fail the lift, which could result in you hurting yourself. So listen up clearly! As you lower yourself down, remember to force your knees out so they track over your feet and don't buckle inwards. We are doing this safely.

As you hit rock bottom keep your midline switched on as your knees stretch reflex will kick-start your upward motion.

Drive up out of the bottom position with knees out and squeeze your glutes at the top to lock out hips.

Aren't squats bad for your knees?

Such a common question that is!

The answer is, only if you have a pre-existing condition or if you perform them incorrectly for months on end. But that's the same with any other exercise if performed incorrectly for long enough. When performed with correct form and to the right depth, squats will actually strengthen your knees.

What's the right depth for squatting?

Many physicians and trainers will argue that doing half squats to parallel is safest for your knees. This doesn't make sense. Your knees are strongest when they are either in a fully extended/flexed position not in between. Plus stopping at parallel (partial squats) only strengthen your quads, while using your full range of motion as nature intended also incorporates your glutes and hamstrings.

Look at Asian cultures where they spend a large portion of their time in a deep squat, working, eating, and socialising. How many children do you know with knee problems? Probably none, but how many children do you see at the playground squatting deep while they play with a toy car or building a sand castle at the beach?

Weightlifters squat deep under tremendous loads and have far fewer knee injuries then other sports. I bet the majority of advocates for partial squats couldn't squat below parallel if they were asked to, hence their stance on the subject. The fact of the matter is we were born with the ability to squat deep but have lost the ability to achieve a good deep squat because of our sedentary lifestyles.

As a qualified chiropractic assistant, I saw that if we don't move it we lose it and a squat is simply something our bodies are designed to do. Take a look at other cultures. They are all squatting to eat, rest, go to the toilet and farm. It's natural.

We are even meant to squat to give birth.

Think of the Paleo concept. Eating Paleo-inspired food means consuming foods you can pick, pluck, hunt and gather. The 'Hunter Gatherer' diet was what we did in the caveman era and when we picked and plucked, we usually did this is a squat position.

Squats will build muscle and strength while increasing your flexibility and surprise surprise, strengthen your knees. Squats are necessary, not only for sport, but for functioning in our daily life. In instances where you may not be able to bend over to pick something up (deadlift) you can always squat.

Another reason the 'Hunter Gatherers' or Asian cultures squat is because it's great for your digestion and bowels. Combine good, real fit food, with regular squats and have healthier elimination!

Dr Damian Kristof came up with this fecal chart to help us see what we can improve on in our diet. After you've had a giggle and pretended to want to turn the page, have a good look and see which 'type' you are!

Forage Fecal Facts Chart

Type № 2.1

Constipation
Too firm and dry, getting stuck on the way out.
Needs more nQ rich foods to relieve the tension.

What to Forage for: A **Forage** breakfast, **more fibre & fluids**

Type № 2.2

Overstaying welcome
Things not moving at the pace they should be.
Got to get things going more quickly and smoothly.

What to Forage for: A **Forage** breakfast, **more fibre & fluids**

Type № 2.3

Close but no cigar
Almost there but needs a little more liquid to smooth things out.
Potentially the result of too many high sugar foods.

What to Forage for: A **Forage** breakfast, **more fluids**

Type № 2.4

And the winner is...
This is what you want to see!
A smooth, solid shape that easily passes through the pipes.

What to Forage for: A **Forage** breakfast, keep up the good work
with your **fibre** and **fluids**

Type № 2.5

Slippery slope
Loosing some control here as things seem to be moving a little too quickly.
Potentially the result of a diet high in soft foods and not enough solids.

What to Forage for: A **Forage** breakfast, **more fibre**

Type № 2.6

Danger zone
Things are traveling too fast here.
Nutrients passing through too quickly to be absorbed.
Potentially a reaction to a food your body doesn't agree with.

What to Forage for: A **Forage** breakfast, **more fibre**

Type № 2.7

Caution, hazardous materials
Moving through far too quickly for any nutrient absorption, something
else is likely to be involved here.
Not to be taken lightly, potentially an infection or other health condition.

What to Forage for: A **Forage** breakfast, **more fibre & fluids, doctor visit**

in nature, find health
Forage

PO Box 466 Hawthorn –VIC 3122 – AUSTRALIA
(03) 9018 6639 – www.foragecereal.com

SO SHUT AND SQUAT!

How to squat

Repeat for 2/3 sets of 8/12 reps. Rest for 60/90 seconds between sets.

Once you're comfortable with squats, you can increase the difficulty by adding weights. Try holding dumbbells at shoulder level, a barbell across your shoulder or a kettle bell at your chest, with both hands and elbows in tight.

Always maintain proper form when doing these.

In the modern world, we are just not able to squat the way other cultures do. For example, the design of modern footwear that often features an elevated or raised heel changes our squat posture. High heel shoes create a shortening of the calf muscles and

Achilles tendon, and a gradual loss of the ankle mobility required to properly do a squat. This often leads people to perform a variation called the Western squat, where the heels remain propped up in the air.

When you're not used to performing a full squat, you'll attempt to squat down, your heels will lift off the floor and you will fall backwards. You can be pretty sure it's because of a loss of flexibility in the ankles.

Three reasons to love the squat!

1. Get more mobile in your ankles

There are many reasons you might have a limited range of motion in the ankles. Wearing high heels is one. However, a common problem with having stiff ankles, may contribute to poor posture. A squat done correctly with the heels flat on the floor needs good flexibility at the ankle and squatting may help improve these conditions.

2. Help decrease back pain

Injuries, high heels, stress and even the birthing process can cause spinal subluxations and lots of people have an excessive curvature in their low back as a result of the pelvis being pulled down in the front by tight hip flexor muscles. During a deep squat the pelvis rotates backward, allowing the spine to elongate. Nice! A long spine and a great neurological stretch! The low back gets a stretch and also creates a traction effect, creating space between the individual segments of the spine.

Improving glutes in a squat helps overall posture. People who squat well have wonderful posture. They stand tall, chest out and the head is correctly aligned so that your ears sit in line with your shoulders. No heads craning forward. You just can't if you're squatting properly.

There are also studies done on why squatting in other cultures is common and in fact not only normal but healthy too.

Take a look at how naturally other cultures do it.

Push-ups

Push-ups are one of the best exercises you can do. They require no equipment, just complete back to basic and simple movements. Our favourite part is that they use a large number of muscle groups and there are hundreds of variations.

So let's get to the set up:

Lie on the floor and put your hands flat on the ground in line with your chest.

Your head stays neutral or tilted slightly up but don't tilt it down. You chest needs to touch the floor. How are you going to get your chest to touch the ground if your head is in the way?

Narrow hand positions will work the triceps harder (goodbye flabby

84

backs of arms) while a wider hand position will have more emphasis on the chest.

Be up on your toes or knees with your hips slightly raised so that the only points of contact with the ground are your toes, chest and hands. This will ensure you keep your core switched on throughout the push-up. Pull in and activate that core.

Make sure your elbows are not flared, as this will put more pressure on your shoulders, just a natural angle about 45 degree angle from your ribs.

Again if you decide to tuck your elbows in to your ribs, this is fine, it'll just put more emphasis on the triceps. From here you press straight up until your arms are locked out. Ensure that your body remains in the same plank position throughout the movements and doesn't start to bow. If it does, this is an indication that your core/trunk strength is weak and will need addressing. Lower yourself back down until your chest touches the ground but hips stay up just enough so your stomach and thighs aren't lying on the floor.

Burpees

Sounds like a pretty horrible name too, right? I often wonder whether the name was given because it's how you feel after doing many of them! The bottom line is, a burpee is a really effective, functional movement and allows you to build strength as well as fitness. The foundation of a burpee is a squat.

So start from standing position and move to a squat and either step down one leg at a time to a push-up position or you may jump both feet back to this position. Then jump both feet back to a standing position.

If you repeat this several times, you can build fitness fast. Do it in lots of ten to begin with. You don't need a gym or a partner. Just pull back the rug or do them in a park while the kids are playing!

Pull-ups vs chin-ups

Aren't they the same thing? Almost. Pull-ups are performed with your hands in a pronated (facing away from you) position, while chin-ups are performed with your hands in a supinated (facing you) position. Both work the back and biceps with a couple of secondary muscle groups being the main differences between the two hand positions.

Chin-ups put a greater emphasis on the biceps. The hand position will also affect the muscles groups involved. A closer grip will work the biceps harder while a wider grip will put more load on the back. If you are going to choose between the two, pull ups are probably a better exercise to do and here's why.

Pull-ups

Pull-ups are a fantastic exercise that uses more than one muscle group and doesn't just focus on the biceps. They can be performed anywhere there is a bar that will support your weight - at the gym, on monkey bars at the park, your doorway or even a tree branch.

Once you've taken your grip, hang from the bar with your arms straight but shoulders are still active. Pull your shoulder blades down and together, don't just hang there loose with your shoulders up around your ears.

Breathe in, keep your torso tight, legs straight and slightly forward of the bar, creating tension in your midline and helping to counter your weight so you don't start swaying. As you pull up, think about raising your chest toward the bar and squeezing your shoulder blades together rather than rounding your back forcing your shoulders forward. Don't put your neck out by reaching for the bar with your chin, it'll get there when it's ready and you're strong enough. Keep your head neutral throughout the movement. Once your chin clears the bar, lower yourself back down to the start position with arms fully extended.

If you're starting out and can't even do one pull-up, practise from a box underneath you and keep trying until you build strength. Rome wasn't built in a day!

Crossfit

So what should you be doing? Well we've talked about constantly varying our exercises, doing shorter, high intensity workouts and sticking to functional movements to save time. Guess what? This is CrossFit in a nutshell.

The Crossfit craze is spreading around the world because it is a brilliant choice for exercise. Crossfit is a combination of gymnastic types of movements, lifting, endurance and squats.

Whether you're an elite athlete training for the Olympics or a grandma that just wants to be able to pick up her grandchild, your needs differ only by degree, not kind. In CrossFit everyone does the same workout, but it's the load and intensity that are scaled to your individual needs.

That's the great thing about CrossFit: everyone learns the same movements and works toward the same goal of finishing each workout. Because workouts can be scaled to every individual's level of fitness, everyone works at the same relative intensity during a workout.

It is not about who finishes first. You're only competing against yourself and trying to better yourself with the help of your teammates around you encouraging you to finish. The sense of community that people share in a CrossFit Box is unrivalled as everyone shares in each other's battles and triumphs on a daily basis building a unique camaraderie.

If you've seen Crossfit, you may think some of the movements look tough. If you are new to CrossFit or wanting to give it a go, most CrossFit boxes run fundamental classes to teach the basic movements in a safe and fun environment before letting you attend the normal CrossFit classes.

I highly recommend you start this way to ensure you have a good understanding of the basic movements before progressing. It's the responsibility of the coach to make sure you are ready to move on and not just throw you in at the deep end.

If you are unsure of anything make sure you ask questions. Every coach has a different teaching style and every person responds differently to those styles so it's about finding a CrossFit box that feels right to you and a coach that you feel comfortable with.

CrossFit in essence is about constantly trying new things. While the majority of your time is spent at your Crossfit box doing Olympic lifting, gymnastics and different forms of cardio, mixing it up with running on the beach, doing a triathlon or playing touch football are all ways to make you 'crossfit'.

Some other great examples of exercises/sports that use functional movements and improve core strength are:

- hiking
- pilates
- martial arts
- BJJ or grappling and wrestling
- intense types of yoga
- surfing

- rock climbing
- dancing
- gymnastics
- swimming
- boot camps

There are many different exercise groups that offer this. Think outdoorsy, nature types of exercise. Variety is essential to keep you interested and your body guessing. It doesn't mean you shouldn't go for a walk around the block or a jog if you feel like it from time to time. Movement is exactly what your body needs. Being fit is one part of being healthy, just as eating fat is another.

So the exercise you choose is just as important as the fat you choose. How much should you exercise? The answer is just as often as you eat good fat: often.

You should choose something that you enjoy too. Think of it like an activity rather than exercise.

I train in martial arts and think of it like learning a skill. That way your mind is focused on the technique, not the fact you are actually exercising. Martial arts is particularly empowering for mind as well as body. When students step on the mat, they are learning a discipline.

It also helps you learn about life and how to apply yourself differently through learning how to defend. It's empowering when you overcome a fear or obstacle through defence and then apply that newfound confidence to fears or obstacles that may have been holding you back in life in general too. It's also a great form of meditation because nothing else is on the mind when you are so focused on the art of defence and technicality of learning a new life skill.

These days we are way too sedentary as we sit in our office jobs at a desk in front of a computer for hours. The type of work we do now has us in a very unnatural position and furthermore, we aren't even getting up from our desks often to walk around and move.

I saw this in practice as a chiropractic assistant witnessing way too many years to the damaging effects on the spine from all the lack of movement, not to mention toxic lifestyle we have been leading.

So get up more every hour from your desk and do some squats for a few minutes. Or at least create a reason to move around!

How important is exercise?

Well, for overall optimal health and function, we really need to move our bodies and spines well. It is through our spines or 'life lines' that we adapt to stress and perceive the world. Our spinal cord, nerves and brain all function every cell, tissue and organ in our body!

Movement runs the brain. It is when we don't move that we start to die. This is why if somebody has had an accident or is in recovery at a hospital that a physical therapist is employed to come and move the patient's legs around for them. We need to keep our bodies moving so that it keeps our brains and nervous systems working.

Exercising is the most underused antidepressant too. We fire off good hormones when we raise our heart beats and break a sweat. Our bodies are just designed to move, and often. It's that simple. And that important.

When we are stressed, the hormone cortisol builds up in our systems.

We go into fight or flight and our heads jut forward in the posture of a boxer. Do this all day every day without releasing the adrenalin and excess cortisol and we land up with a loss of cervical lordosis or backward curve in the neck.

Movement is our body's natural way of moving this out. If cortisol builds up, it becomes toxin within us and can cause a host of issues including fertility troubles and weight gain. During the work day it doesn't necessarily mean you need to get up and sprint every hour. This type of movement could be stretching gently or taking the garbage outside or hanging some washing. But move! Move well and move often.

Then be sure to enjoy your good fats right after your sessions! Fill right up on some quality fat like a handful of almonds or an Amazeball and the recipe is in this book!

Now things are about to escalate. Add good training with good food and you get to shed some weight around the middle section! It doesn't matter how fit you are, you really do make 'abs' in the kitchen. Cut the sugar, dairy, trans fats, wheat, coffee, alcohol and aspartame for a few weeks and just feel the difference!

Gav amounts up the abs

So you want a six-pack but you've got a slab instead? You're doing hundreds of crunches every week, yet the results are nowhere to be seen? While there is a direct correlation between the time you put into cardio and losing weight, the same cannot be said for a good set of abs and how many crunches you do. Some people unfortunately just don't have the genetics to look chiseled out of stone. But for most of us training slightly smarter and eating 'cleaner' will drastically improve our chances of a fit, toned looking stomach, if not a great set of abs.

It's not that you don't have abs, you just can't see them. Everyone has abs. What separates one person from the next is how much fat is covering them. To have a good set of abs on you, men will generally need their body fat percentage to be sub 10%, while ladies will be looking to shave it down to below 18%.

What you put in your mouth has a greater impact on your six-pack than how many crunches you can smash out each morning. You could do 5000 crunches a day and still never have a six-pack as long as you keep thinking donuts are an appropriate pre-workout meal.

Your whole body fat percentage needs to come down and unfortunately   the

abs are usually the last to lose it and the first to regain it. This is going to require a whole lot of discipline and making some serious lifestyle changes if you are to achieve and maintain a great set of abs.

The only way to get abs is through 'clean eating', high intensity cardio and weight training, not just doing isolation crunches every day. You can't just target the fat on your stomach, and that's exactly why all those functional exercises work! They help your fitness and core strength overall.

Your abs, like every other muscle group, need rest days too. They also need variety and a progressive increase in resistance over time to continue to grow and strengthen.

Training schedules can be made up by you depending on what you enjoy and what you feel your body needs. Mix up your routine with reverse crunches, hanging leg raises, planks and weighted sit-ups. There are millions of ab exercises out there and each can be scaled from beginner's level to advanced.

1.   Try new activities: take up a team sport, try wind-surfing, buy a skateboard, learn martial arts or take up dance classes.

2.   Have fun! If you're not excited about an activity then you won't stick with it. If there's no passion, there's no drive, and if there's no drive, there'll be nothing but excuses as to why you can't make it today.

3.   Take rest days.

Crucial fat for fitness

Eating good fat is also extremely essential for the health of our nervous systems. Our nervous systems are the brain, the spinal cord and the nerves that branch off that.

That's a huge amount of life force and 'lifeline', I like to call it, that requires nourishing. Why?

There is something called *myelin*, the protective sheath that covers communicating neurons and is composed of 30% protein and 70% fat. Yes, fat! One of the most common fatty acids in myelin is oleic acid which is also the most abundant fatty acid in human milk and in our diet. No need to bang on again why breast milk is supreme when it comes to rearing children, but here's a little example of how that good fat is fed through to the developing child's brain. On top of this, our diet needs to be A1.

Myelin constitutes the coverings or membranes of neurons/nerves – the specialised brain cells that communicate with each other – and are composed of a thin double-layer of fatty acid molecules. Fatty acids are what dietary fats are composed of. When you digest the fat in your food, it is broken down into fatty acid molecules of various lengths. Your brain then uses these for raw materials to assemble the special types of fat it incorporates into its cell membranes.

Monosaturated oleic acid is the main component of olive oil as well as the oils from almonds, pecans, macadamias, peanuts and avocados. So this is yet another reason to eat them up! Need any more reasons?

Get a chiropractor
If it's optimal health you want and you are really looking to peak your fitness potential, then do so with natural chiropractic. You see, chiropractors are highly trained in the nervous system and their area of expertise is to be able to detect and correct vertebral subluxations (interference to the nerve system) that may send distorted signals to the brain and the rest of the body if your spine is subluxated or misaligned.

Having a scientific, gentle and specific chiropractic adjustment realigns the spine so the communication from brain to body becomes much clearer. It's because your nervous system is the master controller of every other system in the body that I'd like to call it the conductor of the orchestra. Get it right, and your body will be playing beautiful music.

A wave of wellness chiropractors are coming forth though and working with top athletes like Tiger Woods, Lleyton Hewitt and athletic public speaker Anthony Robbins. They all have their own personal chiropractor who travels with them to make sure they're firing off like a well oiled machine. The type of care they receive is holistic and proactive not reactive.

Wellness chiropractors are looking to address the whole body and look for the cause, not just the symptom. They also use objective measures of health to show improvements, like an X-ray, postural test or EMG Scan which is non-invasive and measures nerve system function. It's important to find the right chiropractor so when you acquire one, make sure they can do regular re-examinations that show before and after objective measures of health.

It's really imperative for fitness to have regular chiropractic checks instead of waiting until it's broken to fix it. Muscles are a reactive tissue, not an active issue. This means they don't have a mind of their own. They get told what to do by the nervous system. So when you take pressure off the nerves, with chiropractic care, you're sending a healthier signal to your muscles, which may help with recovery or balance and strength.

The best part is that by having a fully functional nervous system you can also assimilate your nutrition really well. If you have the best nutrition in the world but your nerve system is shot, you may as well be pee-ing it out!

CHIROPRACTIC ERGONOMIC EXERCISES AT THE OFFICE

Healthy posture = less symptoms

These are not designed to treat or correct your posture, but will help prevent a loss of upper cervical lordosis and assist your spine to move well. The main thing is that they're a great neurological stretch which is quite different to other stretches you may be used to. These stretches actually help to restore natural curves in the spine and along with chiropractic care you might achieve some great structural changes.

Exercise 1

Stand with feet hip width apart with knees bent. Press you body against the wall with your chin back, allowing your head to touch the wall. Press your lower spine into the wall too and activate the transverse abdominus. Take pressure off your spinal cord by bringing the head back. If your forward neck shift comes from upper cervical or thoracic spine problems you can still benefit from this stretch.

Exercise 2

Lying on the floor take the foam roller and place it underneath your shoulder blades. Keep your knees bent. Arch over the roller with arms outstretched. Breathe and relax the shoulders.

Those who are not as flexible, place a pillow underneath your neck and work your way up to being able to remove the pillow. Do this stretch for one minute a day and work up to two or three minutes. Roll

over onto your side and get up slowly. We recommend that you see a chiropractor to check your spine and nerve system health while doing these exercises.

Exercise 3

This cat stretch is to be done with your feet together and knees apart. Reach forward and lengthen your spine. Press the pelvis back so you are coming down with your chest first, not your head. Take slow deep breaths and hold for 30 seconds.

For more information

Please contact the Chiropractic Association of Australia's toll free number: 1800-075 003 or visit www.chiropractors.asn.au

Ditch diets!

The 'D' word really is dirty. It's time you start making the food we eat the most powerful form of medicine! Let's call this movement 'mindful eating'. It's now time to make it your lifestyle, not a diet. It's your new way of life that will give you vitality for the long term.

To be able to keep this lifestyle up, it may be challenging at first. Where you shop, what you shop for and what aisles you go to are all about to change. Instead of doing your after-work dash to the supermarket where you know exactly where everything is, you just might be taking your sweet time asking for directions to the 'health food section' and fumbling over backs of packets for a few weeks! Go easy on yourself and know that soon enough, you'll have your little routine back and will be just as quick shopping.

101

I plan to make this even easier though, with a shopping directory for online shopping for the staples, as well as a list of what staples need to be in your pantry and fridge.

The best way to stay wired and inspired though is to surround yourself with like-minded people.

If your friends aren't that into their health, you may like to inspire them and encourage them to join you. It's easier to do things in a group than it is by yourself.

You might just have the best kitchen hands around too, if you have little people living with you. Kids just love having a purpose and doing what grownups do. Get them involved with the cooking. If they're making something with you, chances are they'll be excited to eat it once it's done!

Boom! Little fingers rolling Amazeballs or pressing juice can be great fun, really rewarding and actually a good helping hand.

The most important thing to do to first is start your new food plan now. There no time like the present. By this, I mean, don't wait until your margarine has run out before going to buy the good stuff! Don't say to yourself, "Well, I don't want to waste this full container. I just bought it. When it's finished, then I'll buy butter." No, no, no! Go and have a massive spring clean in your fridge and pantry and get rid of the bad stuff. It's only harming you and stalling you. You are not really saving money, because your health is being compromised in the meanwhile. So get stuck into it!

So get excited about finding new places to shop. There might be a local organic grocer, kitsch health food store or market right near you. It could be fun? You can also get inspired and find new foods at health and food expos. They're always exciting to wander around in. Get creative. Your goal? To have fun eating well because you want to look good, feel good and move well!

"A fit, healthy body—that is the best fashion statement"

— Jess C. Scott

 SHOPPING LIST

Pantry staples

chia seeds - a combination of both black and white are best from Power Super Foods

cartons of nut milk or rice milk

non GMO Bonsoy milk from Spiral Foods

nuts - all types including walnuts, almonds, macadamias and cashews

seeds - a variety of sesame, sunflower and pumpkin (pepitas)

cans of full fat coconut cream

cacao

cacao butter

coconut oil / butter

olive oil - organic and cold pressed

coconut flakes

shredded coconut

dried dates

sultanas

honey

vanilla

apple cider vinegar

seeded mustard

organic dried chick peas, not canned variety

white black-eyed beans

organic tomato pasta sauce - preferably Spiral Foods

xylitol

stevia drops - flavoured from Naturally Sweet

puffed millet

organic peanut butter

tumeric

paprika

cumin

dried oregano

Peruvian Pink Salt from Power Super Foods or any pink salt

black peppercorns

green tea

dandelion tea

herbal tea

almond meal

baking powder

proplenish marine collagen

jar of tahini

rice flour

MSG free vegetable stock powder / cubes

Fridge must haves

mejool dates

organic hormone free, free-range eggs

coconut water

mineral water

fresh mint leaves

anchovies in a glass jar

green vegetables like cucumber, silverbeet, spinach, green beans, broccoli, zucchini, asparagus and brussels sprouts

fresh salmon

avocado

lemon

hormone free red mince meat

hormone free chicken tenderloins

organic butter

garlic

onions

olives

fresh fruit that's in season

sheep's milk or goat's milk yoghurts and cheeses

Freezer back ups

Cocofrio ice cream cartons

frozen raspberries

Spiral Foods do a huge range of gluten free and wheat free crackers which are a perfect snack to throw in a bag! Any nuts and seed combination should always be on hand in a little container and a banana is the perfect fruit to carry because it comes with its very own wrapping - the skin! Another clever protein and good fat snack is a couple of boiled eggs. You can even eat chocolate if it's the good kind, like PANA chocolate which is a nutrient dense, no sugar, no dairy, no additives, high fat, full of good unrefined cacao treat! Whatever your choice, make sure you have something in your bag so you never get stuck with starving!

THROW OUT NOW

margarine

rice bran oil, canola oil, vegetable oil, sunflower oil, grape seed oil

white breads

white wheat flour

sugar

artificial sweetener

sugar free chewing gum

low-fat packaged foods

MSG stocks (look for the words Monosodium Glutamate)

skinny milk

junk foods

FAST FOOL-PROOF
RECIPES
Chapter 7

BREAKFAST IDEAS

THE
BREAKFAST
CAKE

This cake is a really wet one and can stay fresh for a few days. It can be served warm with sheep's milk yoghurt or Cocofrio Ice cream, dolloped on the side. The almond meal provides a gluten-free treat and once again high in protein. This is a twist on the traditional orange and poppy seed cake, but the chia seeds are very high in essential fatty acids. It's a great way of consuming chia seeds.

THE BREAKFAST CAKE

Serves 12

Ingredients

3 lemons - tops removed / cut and scored with a cross about 3cm deep.

6 organic free-range eggs

200g xylitol

250g almond meal

3 ts baking powder

5 tbs soaked chia seeds in a cup of water

Method

Note: *Once you've prepped the lemons, the mixing time is very quick and only takes approx. 8 minutes. Then pop it in the oven with a timer and enjoy the rest of the day!*

Place the prepared lemons in boiling water and simmer for 50 minutes. Remove from the water and purée the whole lemons, including peel, in a food processor, until smooth.

Preheat the oven to 160 °C. In a large mixing bowl, mix the eggs and xylitol until light and fluffy. Add the almond meal and baking powder. Mix until combined. Stir in the lemon purée and soaked chia seeds. Pour the mixture into a 22cm cake tin lined with greaseproof baking paper. Spring tins are best so that it doesn't stick to the bottom and sides. Put the baking paper on the bottom of the tin. Do not use foil.

Bake in the oven for 40 minutes or until firm but still moist. It may need to cook for up to 50 minutes. Leave to cool in the tin for about 5 minutes then turn onto a wire rack and cool there.

CAVEMAN CEREAL
Serves 8

Ingredients

4 cups of puffed millet or amaranth

1 cup of macadamia nuts

1 cup of cranberries

2 cups of coconut flakes

1 cup of pepitas

1 cup of slivered almonds

Method

Mix into a snap lock container and serve with nut milk, rice or coconut milk or for extra protein, goat's milk and a dollop of hard set sheep's milk yoghurt.

CAVEMAN
CEREAL

KALE
OMELETTE

KALE OMELETTE
Serves 2

Ingredients

· ·

4 - 6 eggs

1 Spanish / purple onion

5 large kale leaves

1 tbs coconut oil

Pinch of salt

Dash of Spiral Foods
tamari sauce (optional)

· ·

Method

Pre-prepare the eggs and whisk them in a bowl, adding salt and tamari.
Chop onion and kale and fry in oil in a heated pan. Add the eggs, let
them cook and flip to fry the other side. Serve with goats cheese or
avocado.

SNACKS

HUMMUS

HUMMUS
Serves 6

Ingredients

. . . .

1 jar of hulled tahini
(the lighter coloured
one: Spiral Foods
recommended)

Peruvian Pink salt

1 large clove of garlic

1 whole juice of a lemon

1 can of rinsed and
drained organic chick
peas

Paprika, Parsley and extra
virgin organic olive oil to
garnish

. . . .

Method

Empty the whole jar of tahini into a food processor. Fill the jar with water, filtered if you can, and add it to a food processor with crushed garlic clove and blend until it changes to a whiter or lighter colour. Add salt and lemon juice and blend again.

Taste and see if it needs more salt or lemon. Add the chick peas. Decide if you need water or more lemon juice. Pour into a bowl and sprinkle paprika, drizzle oil to keep it moist because this can be kept in the fridge for a couple of days. When you have it in the food processor you can also add parsley to garnish or even a bunch to mix through. Parsley helps to take away the strong garlic flavour by working from the gut.

118

CHIA SEED BREAD

Serves 3 or 4

Ingredients

. . . .

¾ cup of rice flour or quinoa flour or coconut flour

1 cup almond meal

2 tbs chia seeds

3 eggs

2 tbs apple cider vinegar

1 tbs baking powder

Pinch of Peruvian Pink Salt or sea salt

I cup of water

. . . .

Method

Sift flour and almond meal into a bowl, soak chia seeds in a half a cup of water for a few minutes add gel like chia seeds, eggs, and the rest of ingredients and mix.

Pour into a baking paper lined small loaf tin. Put in a pre-heated oven for 25 - 30 mins on 175 °C.

Serve with organic butter or coconut butter. Also you could eat with organic peanut butter for extra fat and protein. Other fat spreads are things like goat's cheese or avocado. For kids parties, find additive and colouring free sprinkles from your local health foods shop.

CHIA SEED
BREAD

BRUSSEL
SPROUT CHIPS

BRUSSEL SPROUT CHIPS

Serves 4

Ingredients

½ tbs Peruvian Pink Salt
or sea salt

About 12- 20 brussel
sprouts

Olive oil

Method

Cut all Brussel sprouts into halves and place on a lined baking tray.

Sprinkle with salt and drizzle with oil and put in an oven on 180°C for about 30-40 mins or until golden and crunchy on the outside and softish on the inside.
Yum!

PALEO CRACKERS

Serves 4

Ingredients

½ cup each of 3 different types of seeds, which can be sesame, pepitas (pumpkinseeds), chia seeds or sunflower seeds

1 cup almond meal

1½ cups of water

Pinch of Peruvian Pink Salt or sea salt

1 clove of crushed garlic

Fresh herbs if you choose for extra flavour

Method

Mix all ingredients in a bowl. Let it soak up some of the water through the chia seeds. It should look a little wet. Place in a lined baking tin tray with baking paper, not foil. Spread evenly so it looks about 0.5cm thin, push to the edges to create a square edge. Put in oven for 25 mins at 175°C then make marks to be able to divide into squares. Put back in oven for about 10 mins and then let edges brown.

Serve with avocado, goat's feta, tomato, organic peanut butter or organic butter.

Keep in a snap lock container.

123

PALEO
CRACKERS

CAULI
FLOWERS

CAULI FLOWERS
Serves 2-4

Ingredients

1 whole cauliflower

A few drops of Spiral foods Tamari sauce

1 tbs cumin powder

½ tsp Peruvian Pink Salt or sea salt

2 large organic free range eggs

2 tbs of coconut oil

Sesame seeds

Method

Wash and cut cauliflower pieces into small flowerettes. Slightly boil them for about 5 minutes so they don't go too soft but they're defiantly not so hard. Whisk eggs into a bowl with other ingredients and dip cauliflowers into and then fry into a pan with coconut oil. Move them around so it is fried on several sides. Eat straight away or eat cold the next day if stored in an airtight container.

DINNERS & LUNCHES

MOROCCAN
SPICED
CHICKEN

MOROCCAN SPICED CHICKEN

Serves 3

Ingredients

500/600g organic hormone free, free range chicken tenderloins

2 heaped tbs coconut oil

1 heaped tbs of turmeric

1 heaped tbs of cumin

Pinch of Peruvian Pink Salt or sea salt

Method

Throw the pieces of chicken in a pan with the oil, then sprinkle the spices over the chicken on the upside. Wait til cooked then turn and cook other side. Serve with some coleslaw you mix with high fat mayonnaise that's preservative and additive free or make your own and store, then use daily.

GREEN BEAN AND BROCCOLI SALAD

Serves 4

Ingredients

· ·

A bowl full of green beans
and broccoli or broccolini

1 whole lemon

Pinch of Peruvian Pink
salt or sea salt

1 tbs seeded mustard

2 tbs olive oil

· ·

Method

Put all greens into a massive bowl. Boil the kettle and fill up the bowl
with boiling water. Pour the water over the greens to blanch or par-
boil them. Cover with a large plate to keep the steam in. Leave for 5-10
minutes. Drain and rinse. To make the dressing, squeeze the juice of
the lemonade other ingredients into. Glass, stir and drizzle over the
greens. Best served cold with a piece of salmon.

GREEN
BEAN AND
BROCCOLI
SALAD

PASTA
FREE
BOLOGNESE

PASTA FREE BOLOGNESE

Serves 4

Ingredients

. . . .

500g organic hormone-free mince meat

1 whole onion diced

1 jar of organic additive free pasta sauce (Spiral Foods is recommended)

Half a cauliflower

2 tbs dried oregano

1 grated zucchini

Pinch of Peruvian Pink Salt or sea salt

Cracked black pepper

2 heaped tbs coconut oil

. . . .

Method

Break off pieces of cauliflower into boiling water and let it cook for about 5-8 mins. Fry up the onion in the coconut oil in a pan, add meat and zucchini and keep stirring, making sure meat is browned. Add oregano and salt, pepper and pasta sauce. Drain cauliflower and stir through. Serve immediately or store in airtight containers and eat for next meal.

SWEET TREATS

CHIA
PUDDING

CHIA PUDDING

Ingredients

½ cup of chia seeds

1½ cups of coconut milk
or nut milk

¼ cup of berries or
pomegranate or banana -
something to top it with

Stevia drops to taste

Coconut syrup to taste

1 tbs cacao powder from
Power Super Foods

Method

Place all ingredients into a large mixing bowl and stir. Allow seeds to soak up liquid. The chia will become like a gel. Serve into bowls or glasses and top with fruit or Cocofrio ice cream. You may store in airtight container too for a few days.

138

COCOFRIO ICE CREAM SPIDER

Serves 1

Ingredients

. . . .

Mango or Salted Caramel
Cocofrio ice cream

Mineral or soda water

. . . .

Method

Take a heaped ice cream scoop size of Cocofrio ice cream and put it in a tall glass. Fill the glass with Mineral or soda water. The bubbles will give it a nice froth. You can decorate the glass with a paper umbrella or a strawberry. Trial other Cocofrio flavours. Stir a little before drinking. Best eaten with a spoon as well as a straw.

COCOFRIO
ICE CREAM
SPIDER

CHOCCY NUTTY
CRUNCH

CHOCCY NUTTY CRUNCH

Serves 6

Ingredients

. . . .

¾ cup of cacao butter

1 cup coconut oil

1½ tbs cacao powder

3 tbs coconut syrup or 2 tbs agave syrup

. . . .

Method

Melt the cacao butter and coconut oil in a small pan, add and stir in the cacao powder, then mix in the syrup. Leave aside. Place a sheet of baking paper on a dinner-sized plate and sprinkle almonds, coconut flakes and frozen berries all over evenly.

Pour over the melted chocolate from the outside in and it will run and move toward the centre. Make sure all pieces are covered in some of the melted liquid/ chocolate so that it can all be held together once set.

Put it in the freezer for 2 hours to set. Remove from freezer about 20-30 minutes before eating. Break triangle pieces off to serve, then eat right away!

142

CUKE AND PINE ICY-POLES
Serves 6

Ingredients

· ·

Half a pineapple   ¼ cup coconut cream

1 Lebanese or smaller size
cucumber

· ·

Method

Wash cucumbers and cut up pineapple. Juice in preferably a juicer that squashes or masticates the fruit and vegetables so the enzymes are killed by the heat of the engine in other conventional juicers.

Pour in coconut cream and then into BPA free icy pole containers and freeze overnight! Eat whenever you're needing a pick me up cold thirst quencher!

143

CUKE
AND PINE
ICY-POLES

FESTIVE FOODS

AMAZEBALLS

AMAZEBALLS
Makes 12-15 balls

Ingredients

2 cups quinoa oat flakes, Forage porridge (gluten free options) or rolled oats

1 cup pitted dates, roughly chopped

½ cup of shredded coconut

½ cup of sultanas

½ cup of almonds

2 tbs organic peanut butter

1 tbs cocoa powder

2 tbs honey

¾ tbs water

1 ts vanilla extract

Method

Put all ingredients apart from the water into a food processor and blend until it has the consistency of breadcrumbs. Add the water and continue to process until it becomes sticky enough to roll into balls. Use a tablespoon to measure the mixture and roll into firm balls. Roll into desiccated coconut to make the outside look pretty and store in an airtight container in the fridge.

Note: You'll need to make sure the peanut butter is a good quality, pesticide-free kind. Spiral Foods do a great one. If your guests are anaphylactic and cannot consume peanuts, you may like to use a different type of nut butter or cold-pressed organic coconut oil instead.

148

CACAO SLICE

Ingredients

3 cups of walnuts

1 cup of raw cacao

½ cup dried cranberries

2½ cups of pitted medjool dates

¼ tsp salt

½ cup cacao butter from Power Super Foods

Method

In a food processor, pulse walnuts and cacao butter until roughly chopped. Add the cacao, salt and pulse several times to combine. Add the dates one at a time until the mixture resembles bread crumbs. Add cranberries.

Line a tray with baking paper in a slice tin and pack mixture firmly inside, pressing down until it resembles a slice. Set in fridge for 20 minutes. Cut into small squares and sprinkle with cacao to serve.

Notes

Use cacao to add to the goodness of walnuts. In its raw form, cacao is a super food high in many mineral and vitamins. It doesn't end there – cacao is like an atomic bomb of feel good food that helps release happy hormones and is actually packed with protein too. You could add so many ingredients to personalise these, such as freeze-dried strawberries or blueberries.

CACAO
SLICE

DRINKS

CHOCOLATE
CASHEW
MILK

CHOCOLATE CASHEW MILK

Serves 2

Cashew milk is the creamiest of homemade nut milks and the most refreshing. Since the nuts blend entirely into the water, no nuts go to waste in the process, which also means that the cashew milk retains all the fibre and nutrients in the cashews. This recipe is to be made with a Kuvings or any other compatible cold-pressed juicer.

Ingredients

Make 2 cups of cashew milk (400g)

1 tbs Spiral Foods Honey

1 tbs raw Cacao Powder from Power Super Foods

A sprinkle of cinnamon

Method

Rinse cashews well and soak them in water for at least 3 hours.

Using a large spoon or ladle, carefully measure out the mixture into the Kuvings Whole Slow Juicer, making sure to add equal parts cashew and water each time. Finish by straining out the cashew flesh using a strainer or cheesecloth.

Add Power Super Foods cacao which is a great source of antioxidants and it contains an abundance of magnesium, iron and protein. Pour all ingredients together into the blender. Add cinnamon as a garnish.

154

THE LSD
Serves 1

This fun feel-good drink stands for 'Long Soy Dandelion'. It's a bit if a pun because Dandelion is excellent for the digestive system and a nice warm cup of this will certainly get your body buzzing with love.

Ingredients

½ cup of Spiral Foods Bonsoy

Boiling water

2 teaspoons of Dandelion granules

1 teaspoon of xylitol or stevia drops to taste

Method

Add the dandelion in a cup to boiling water, don't fill all the way and add the non GMO creamy Bonsoy. Sweeten with the rest of the ingredients to taste.

THE LSD

CHOC-MINT TEA

CHOC-MINT TEA

Serves 1

Ingredients

. . . .

Peppermint tea bag or
fresh mint leaves

Boiling water

1-2 chocolate flavoured
stevia drops to taste

. . . .

Method

Make the cup of tea as per usual and the chocolate flavoured stevia
adds flavour as well as sweetness.

COCO COFFEE

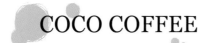

Simply add 1 scoop of Cocofrio ice cream in your favourite flavour to a shot of your favourite coffee.

It's a great sweetener alternative and adds good fats to your day! Remember, these good fats help you to full fuller, longer and it tastes divine!

Terms

ts = teaspoon
tbs = tablespoon
SR flour = self-raising flour

COCO
COFFEE

REFERENCES & RECOMMENDED EXTRA READING

Cordian, L. (2002) **The Paleo Diet**. Hoboken, New Jersey. Wiley.

Fife, B and Kabara, Jon J. **The Coconut Oil Miracle**. Avery Trade

Gedgaudas, N. (2009) **Primal Body, Primal Mind**. 2nd Edition. Rochester, Vermont. Healing Arts Press.

Gullespie, D. (2010) **The Sweet Poison Quit Plan**. Melbourne, Australia. Penguin.

Gullespie, D. (2010). **Sweet Poison**. Penguin.

Kringoudis, N. (2012). **Fertilise Yourself**. Melbourne, Australia. ini-inspire.

Orr. A. (2007). **Concept Shen Seminar Notes**. Melbourne, Australia. Shen Therapies.

Sipser, W & Lew, A. (2008). **7 Things Your Doctor Forgot to Tell You**. Rockpool Publishing

Ten Bosch, Laurentine, *www.foodmatters.tv/articles* and *www.drmercola.info*

Wilson, S. *http://www.sarahwilson.com.au/2011/03/caveman-exercise-a-why-and-how-rundown/*

Wilson, S (2012). **I Quit Sugar**.

162

You may be a little lost at first with where to shop and find these new pantry items. We want to make it easy to incorporate this healthy way of eating fit into your lifestyle.

At your local shopping centre most supermarkets now have an organic and health food section or aisle. Be warned though and read the backs of packets. You can find your organic fresh produce there, however, shop at local farmers markets too. Sugar alternatives are found in the sugar sections too with xylitol and stevia blends available right there at the supermarket. Be warned which brands to look out for by once again reading the nutrition column and avoiding the additives and other nasties mentioned in the book.

Your wheat-free baking flours may be in the health food section, and when choosing eggs, try to look for organic, not just free range, so you can be sure the chickens have been fed a natural diet free of hormones, pesticides or antibiotics. A great egg-free alternative for vegans is soaked chia seeds. Log onto Power Super Food's website for more information on how to use it. See below for the website address.

More and more little health stores are popping up that will stock your organic cold-pressed coconut oils, sugar free alternatives, wheat free flours and dairy alternatives. Try to buy the staples bulk and on line and then get fresh ingredients wherever is convenient and fun. If it's in season, chances are it'll be cheaper too.

SHOPPING DIRECTORY

SHAPE UP AND SHOP HERE

Sipser Family Chiropractic
Wellness Centre
20 Ormond Rd Elwood, VIC 3184
03-95313131
www.chiro4life.com

The Pagoda Tree
2/124 Bridport Street West, Albert
Park VIC 3206
(03) 9686 7454
www.thepagodatree.com.au

Forage Cereal
PO Box 466 Hawthorn VIC 3122
 p: +61 03 9018 6639
www.foragecereal.com

Ward's Gym
Callum and Gavin Ward
4 York St, Richmond, Victoria 3121
Mbl 0417370878
www.wardsgym.com

Cocofrio Ice Cream
www.cocofrio.com
yum@cocofrio.com.au

Power Super Foods
ww.powersuperfoods.com.au

Kuvings Juicers
www.kuvings.net.au

Spiral Foods Pty Ltd
this earth, this food...
www.spiralfoods.com.au
info@spiralfoods.com.au
www.bonsoy.com
Info@bonsoy.com

Alkaline World
Be healthy, naturally!
30 Fabio Court, Campbellfield Vic
3061
Mobile 0422 111 111
Phone 03 9357 1777
 www.alkalineworld.com.au

Activewear Brazil
info@activewearbrazil.com.au
Phone: (+61) 0402 564 669

**Lifestyle, Food & Wellness
Coach course**
www.wellnesscoachingaustralia.com.au
Fiona Crosgrove - Director
Wellness Coaching Australia
PO Box 194,
Nobby Beach 4218, Australia
Phone: +61 2 8006 9055
Fax: +61 2 07 5526 6767
info@wellnesscoachingaustralia.com.au

COCOFRIO

DAIRY & GLUTEN FREE
ICE CREAM ALTERNATIVE

Cocofrio organic
dairy-gluten-and
fructose-free
coconut milk ice
cream is stirring up
a flavourlution

www.cocofrio.com.au

Combine a zest for life and health with a love of wholesome food and flavours and you reach to the heart of Cocofrio, our official sponsors.

Launched in 2013, Cocofrio's vision is to offer good food and ice-cream lovers the creamiest, tastiest and healthiest organic coconut ice cream in Australia. In less than 12 months, they've established themselves as Australia's favourite organic coconut milk ice cream producer. And stocking with retailers around Australia, word is spreading fast.

Why Cocofrio as sponsorship partner?

The answer starts with Cocofrio as a company. Here's how they answered the questions that convinced us they were the perfect partners for Eat Fat Be Thin.

What's so special about Cocofrio?

Cocofrio subscribes to the proven belief that we are what we eat. After years of health and dietary research, we really began to understand the extraordinary properties of the coconut.

We love a healthy way of life. But we hate having to sacrifice enjoyment and flavour in our favourite treat. That's what led us to product trials and recipe and flavor experiments using coconut milk as the basis for a delicious new range of dairy- gluten- and fructose-free organic coconut ice cream.

We figured that if you eat what you love, love what you eat AND know it's miles healthier than any other form of ice cream, you'd leap at the product.

Why coconut milk instead of ordinary dairy milk?

The old saying 'eat fat get fat' doesn't apply to coconut milk as it does to dairy icecream which, of course, is mostly animal fat.

Cocofrio coconut milk ice cream products are crammed with what are known as medium chain fatty acids.

In simple terms, your body immediately converts these fatty acids to energy rather thanstoring them in your system as fat. If you don't have the right mix of a healthy, right fat diet, rigorous exercise and even potentially preventative drugs, animal fats like those in dairy ice cream can place you at risk of high cholesterol, arterial flow reduction and coronary disease.

On the other hand, Cocofrio ice cream has omega 6 fatty acids that are strongly connected to better heart health.

What other benefits does coconut milk ice cream have?
The list is long:

- Coconut milk is high in lauric acid, one of the active components in human breast milk. It's a key contributor to the formation of a stable immune system, as well as blood elasticity.
- An average serving of coconut milk can provide 22 percent of our daily iron needs.
- It contains above average levels of vitamins C, E, B1, B3, B5 and B6 as well calcium, magnesium, phosphorus, selenium and sodium.
- Anti-oxidant elements also help in the fight against free radicals.

How is Cocofrio ice cream sweetened?
Cocofrio is committed to peak human health. All components of our ice cream are certified organic by Australia's leading organic certification agency, Australian Certified Organic (ACO). These include our organic brown rice malt syrup with which we sweeten our products.

The syrup is organically pure, fructose-free and low GI. It comprises 50 percent soluble complex carbohydrates (maltotriose), 45 percent maltose, and three percent glucose.

Your body digests the maltose in 1.5 hours and the complex carbohydrates in three.You absorb the small quantity of glucose immediately. That means a slow and controlled energy release, consistent blood sugar levels, and an even energy flow, with none of the adverse effects on the bloodstream of other sweeteners.

Visit **www.cocofrio.com.au** for more detail on products, flavours, health and diet information, where to buy, and how to become a stockist.

SPIRAL FOODS

Started in the 70's in Melbourne, Australia with a group of alternates, Spiral Foods company had a desire to follow the Macrobiotic way of life. Since then we have seen many changes in eating patterns and fads but Spiral has maintained its roots.

TODAY...

Spiral Foods is Australia's leading supplier of quality Traditional Foods with an emphasis on organics. We are now in our fourth decade and our products are found nationally in Australia, New Zealand, South East Asia, Japan, US and Colombia.

Our range includes the finest Organic Oils and Vinegars, Traditional foods of Japan, Canadian Maple syrup, Mexican Agave, Organic Fruit Juices & Purees from the US, readymade organic sauces & drizzles and a large range of local Australian quality groceries.

At Spiral Foods we are proud of our contributions to help slow the unnecessary changes that are occurring to our earth, climate and oceans. Our products are made by people with a passion for wholesome traditional foods of the highest standards and quality.

Good, safe, wholesome food is a basic human right. Our foods continue to provide nourishment and well-being across the generations of people who take care about the food they eat and our earth. We believe good safe wholesome food is a basic human right.
this earth, this food . . .

SPIRAL · FOODS · A · NATURAL

POWERSUPERFOODS

I highly recommend Power Super Foods for all your salt, chia seeds and cacao as well as other complete super-foods!

They're not only a wonderful company, but they make quality products. Don't just take our word for it! Here's their promise to you:

Since 2001, Power Super Foods is Australia's premier source for the finest organic products specialising in organic, vegan, raw, Low GI, fairly traded, paleo, gluten-and-dairy-free functional foods.....our drive to lead the industry in introducing these unique foods to the Australian marketplace is appreciated by health conscious consumers around the country. We have traveled the globe (30+ countries !!) absorbing the ancient wisdom and searching for unique, traditional plants that provide energy and enhance wellbeing; we invite you to experience something new and enjoy adding these healthy traditions to your modern lifestyle, and will continue to introduce more and more intriguing functional foods and products as they come to our attention.

Our premium quality "superfoods" are always free of artificial preservatives or colours, and free of synthetic flavourings or additives helping you to meet your nutritional needs deliciously, naturally, and simply. We source our premium products through partnerships with farming communities around the world and pay a fair price to create economic opportunities among indigenous people in developing countries, supporting native agricultural traditions and helping to expand the development of good organic farming practices globally. Certified organic means they are grown without the application of petrochemical fertilisers or chemical pesticides, and are non-GMO and non-irradiated....the absence of all these elements speaks to the purity of the products.

This 100% Australian-owned company is committed to socially and environmentally responsible business practices, including hybrid company cars and carbon offsets every year. Part profits are donated annually to amazing organisations around the world devoted to changing this planet for the better in important arenas like endangered wildlife rehabilitation, empowering disadvantaged women, Tibetan causes, rainforest replanting, green energy & transport, etc. Power Super Foods is very proud to be a green, sustainable, progressive and planet-friendly business.

gourmetperuvianpinksalt

Peruvian Pink Salt has been hand harvested for over 2000 years from a natural ancient ocean spring bubbling up to the surface in theSacred Valley of the Incas near Machu Picchu, Peru at around 4000 metres above sea level. Pure salt sources are scarce today due to pollution of land and sea – ours is a low carbon footprint, evaporated product (not mined) and is carefully tested against heavy metal contamination.

This is the perfect healthy seasoning with a prized robust flavour and the rich mineralization creates a lovely pale pink colour, containing so many trace minerals including calcium, iron, potassium, magnesium, copper and zinc. The terraced salt ponds are owned by over 380 individual indigenous families, so why not enjoy gourmet quality flavour while assisting traditional local communities?

Serving suggestion: *Ideal for both gourmet cooking and everyday nutritional food preparation...great on just about everything! Check out our website for delicious healthy recipes where gourmet salt is a featured ingredient.*

KUVINGS JUICERS

Kuvings & NUC International Awards Winner for innovation.

Kuvings is leading with the latest technology. Kuvings Silent Juicer has been widely recognised by the International Invention Fair for its advanced technology.

A cold press juicer gently presses fruits and vegetables rather than high speed grinding and chewing, which helps keep the nutrients and enzymes intact and alive. These valuable enzymes transform the juice into liquid that helps your digestion; assisting the body to absorb the nutrients, effectively boosting your energy level and immune system, and can also assist in healing your cells for good health – especially when drinking green vegetable juice! This means, no more separation in your juice.

J.M.C.S. (Juicer Module Comprising System)'s PATENTED low-speed masticating technology squeezes and extracts juice maintaining all the nutrients that are 100% pure.

Cold Press Juicing

Drinking Juice – Cold Press Fruit Juice will increase your energy levels. Vegetable Juice is essential to regenerate the cells in your body. 67% of all nutrients and enzymes are absorbed into your body within 15 minutes when you drink cold press juice from a Slow Juicer compared to 17% when you eat raw fruit and vegetables.

Semi-permanent and Eco-friendly Material

The strainer and juicing screw are made with Ultem, eco-friendly material, which allows you to extract more natural tasting juice. The Ultem, used at NASA, is eco-friendly material due to its durability and heat resistance. Strainer: Micro filter, Stainless Steel Mesh. The juice is filtered through the micro filter and results in optimal taste.

The strainer is where the juice is separated from the pulp. Once you put the fruit and vegetables through the chute, it gets squeezed and pressed by the auger which in turn squeezes the juice into the strainer holes and pushes the pulp via the wipers into the pulp hole in the strainer.

Ultem is just one of the highest quality material used in the Kuvings Cold Press Juicer hence why they have won so many international awards.

Easy clean up after juicing

Kuvings has made cleaning very simple. Using the juice cap, pour water through the juicer, turn the motor on and allow it to self clean before pulling it apart to give all parts a thorough clean. For perfect juice every time it is important to clean your juicer properly. By drying your juicer parts with a towel after washing you can eliminate juice residue staining and pulpy juice in the future.

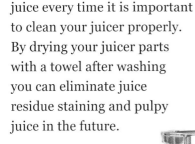

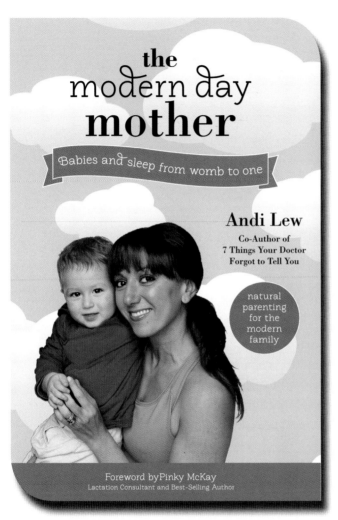

the
modern day
mother

Babies and sleep from womb to one

Andi Lew

Co-Author of
**7 Things Your Doctor
Forgot to Tell You**

natural
parenting
for the
modern
family

Foreword by Pinky McKay
Lactation Consultant and Best-Selling Author

**A guide to natural parenting
for the modern family**

• Easier pregnancy and birth
• Losing post baby weight
• Sleep solutions without tears
• Paediatric chiropractic
• Infant massage & bonding
• Understanding breastfeeding

"Strong evidence-based, it's
beautifully supportive."

*Pinky McKay, Lactation
Consultant, best-selling
author*

"Such a gentle, lovely way of
giving advice. It's the charm of
the book."

*Suzanne Male, journalist &
author*

"Andi presents Attachment
Parenting in an easy-to-
understand way."

*Dr Bill Sears, best-selling
author*

**Buy in e-book and paperback at
www.themoderndaymother.com
Also available for the Kindle at
Amazon.com and from the Apple iBookstore**

How healthy are you?

Discover seven key things your doctor may have forgotten to tell you, including what you can incorporate into your lifestyle to achieve optimal health.

"The knowledge that lies within will certainly impact your thinking and empower your life."

Dr John F. Demartini

Available as an e-book and paperback from

www.7things.com.au

Also available from Amazon.com

7 THINGS YOUR DOCTOR FORGOT TO TELL YOU

DR WARREN SIPSER and ANDI LEW
Foreword by Dr John Demartini
Contributor of the International Bestseller *THE SECRET*
Author of the multiple Bestseller *COUNT YOUR BLESSINGS*

A GUIDE FOR OPTIMAL HEALTH